In appreciation of the countless color and art lovers
who gently participated in the crazy world of
coloring and calming activity.

- Mayank Patel

Author has wisely selected faces of known celebrities and created these 60 Illustrations in
light shade to provoke your shading and coloring skills.

In the Shading and Coloring Book, you'll enjoy 60 exclusive hand drawn sketches, from
Hollywood actors, music celebrities to international athletes. You'll surely provoke your
imagination, rendering and color senses.

Spread out your imagination and creative mind to occupy in the pleasurable activity.

Each Page is designed for fun and Relaxations, Choice of coloring kits can be utilized
(color pens, color pencils, crayons, water colors, ink colors).

Adults and older kids who enjoy coloring can use this special and exclusive
shading book based on features of the faces.

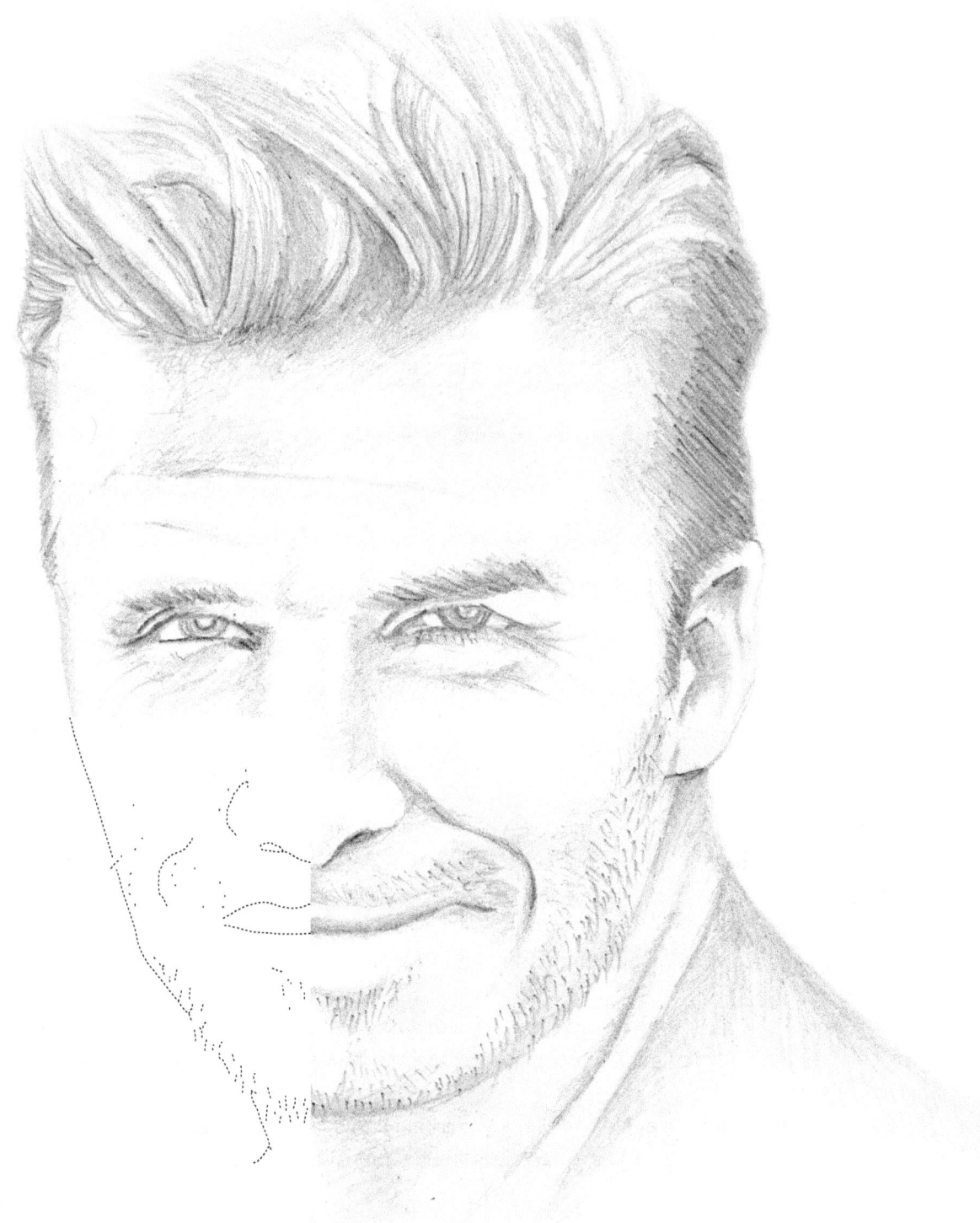

You can enjoy countless possibilities with coloring tools — why edge to flat coloring? Alternatively, practice and enjoy different types of coloring techniques. With a little trial and practice, you'll control them in no time. Indeed, you'll be adding shade, light and a whole lot of aesthetics to your work piece.

Shading with coloring tools is fun. It adds depth to any sketch and explores the range of a small number of colors to multiple variations.

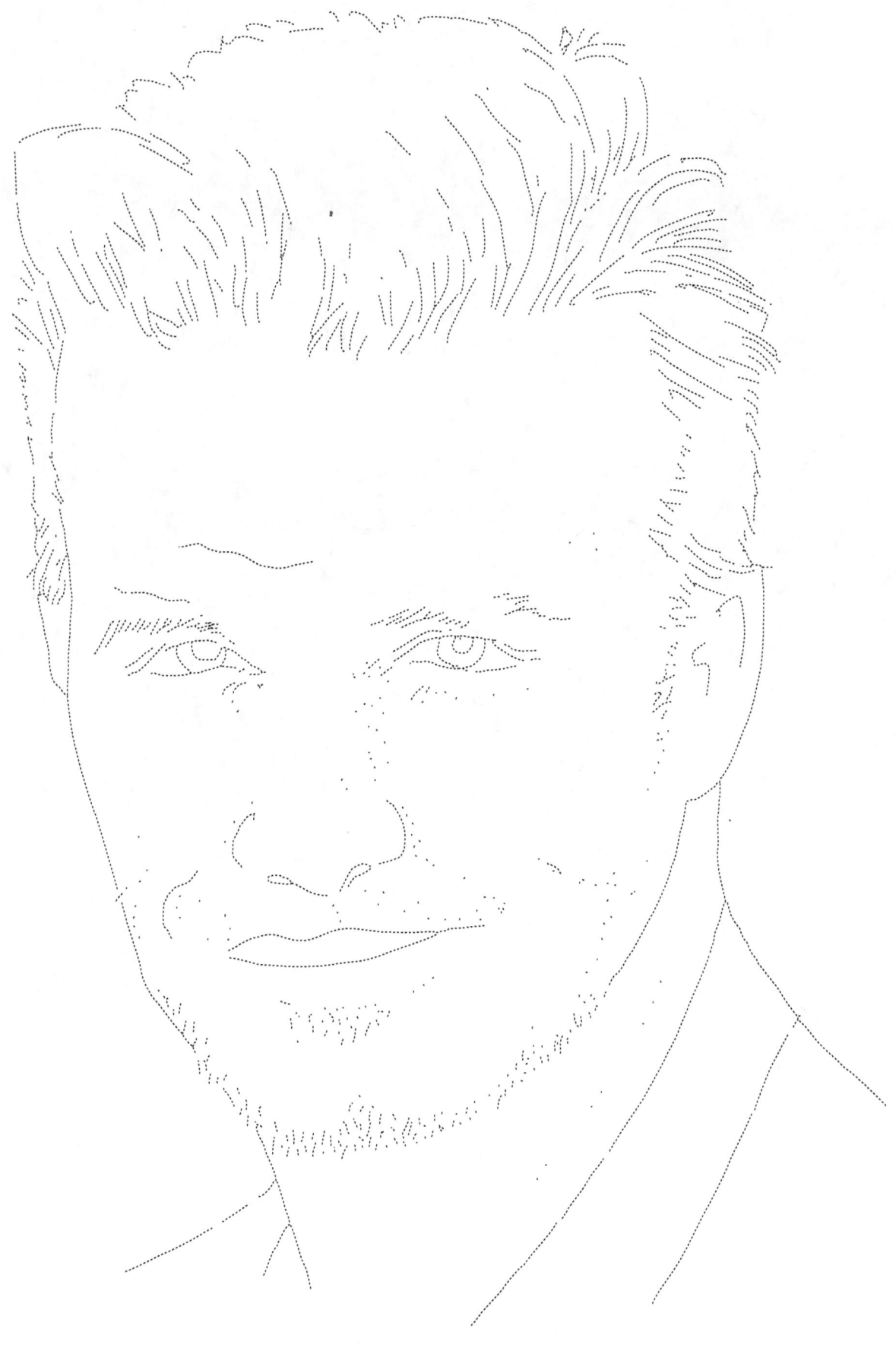

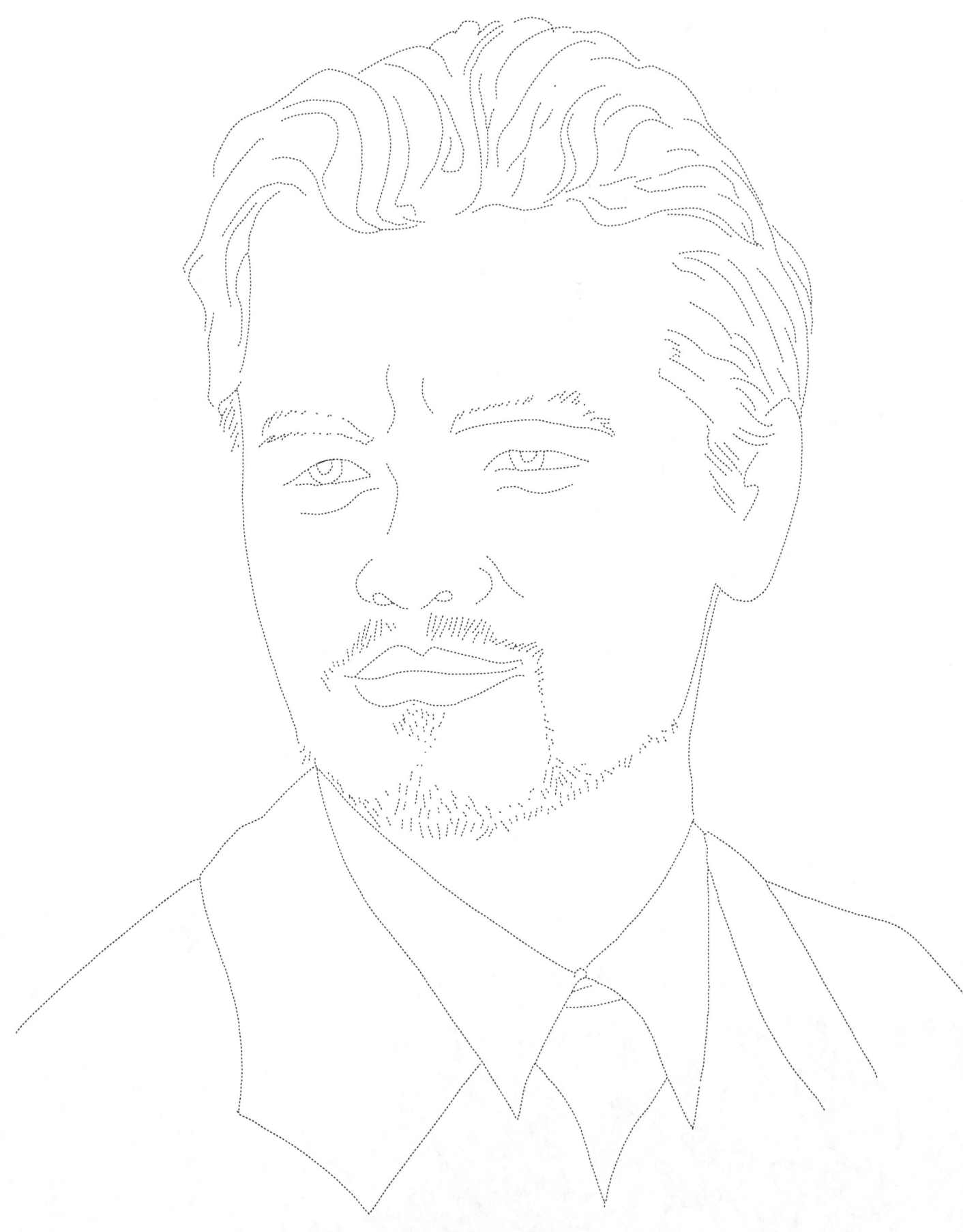

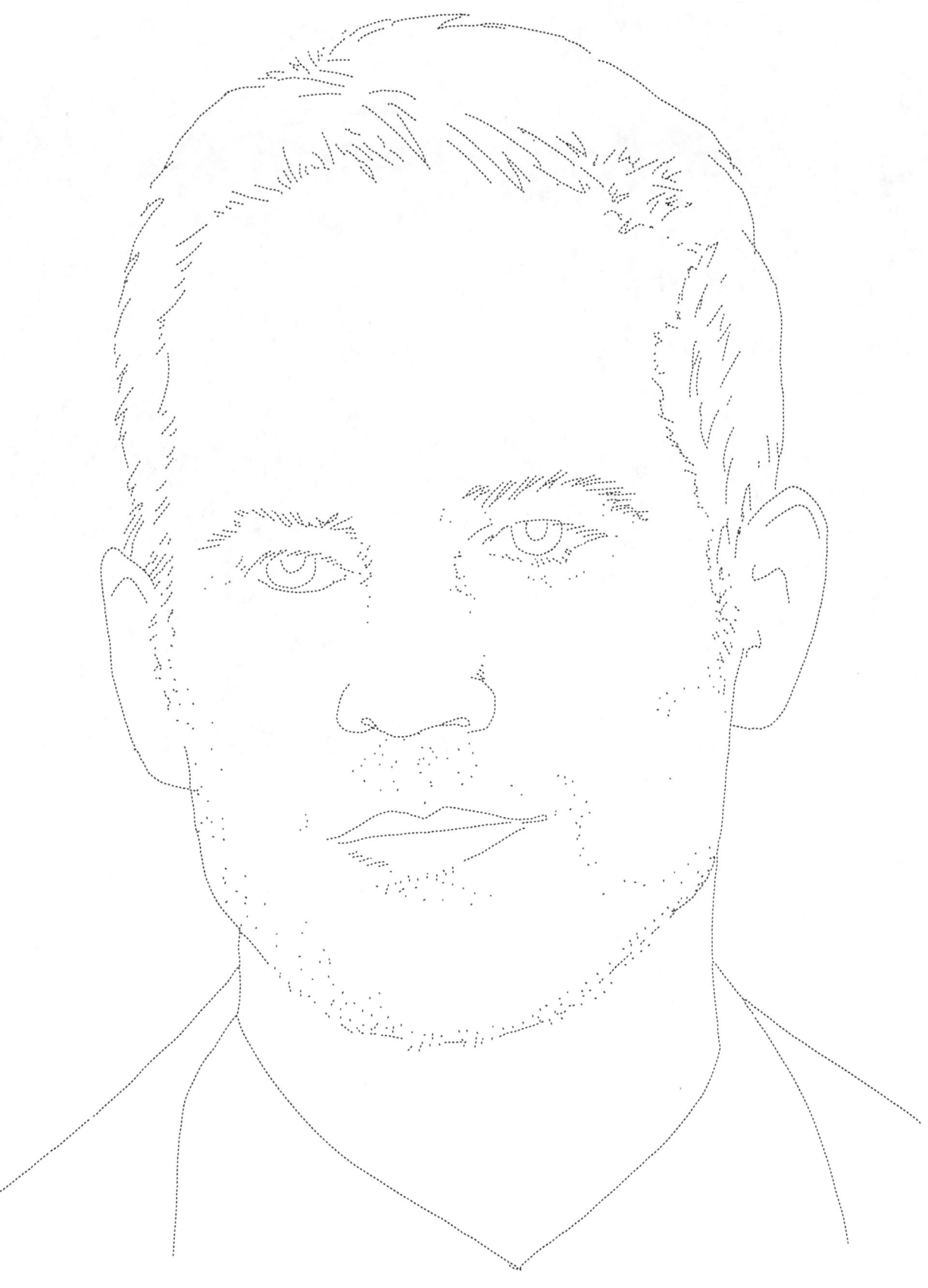

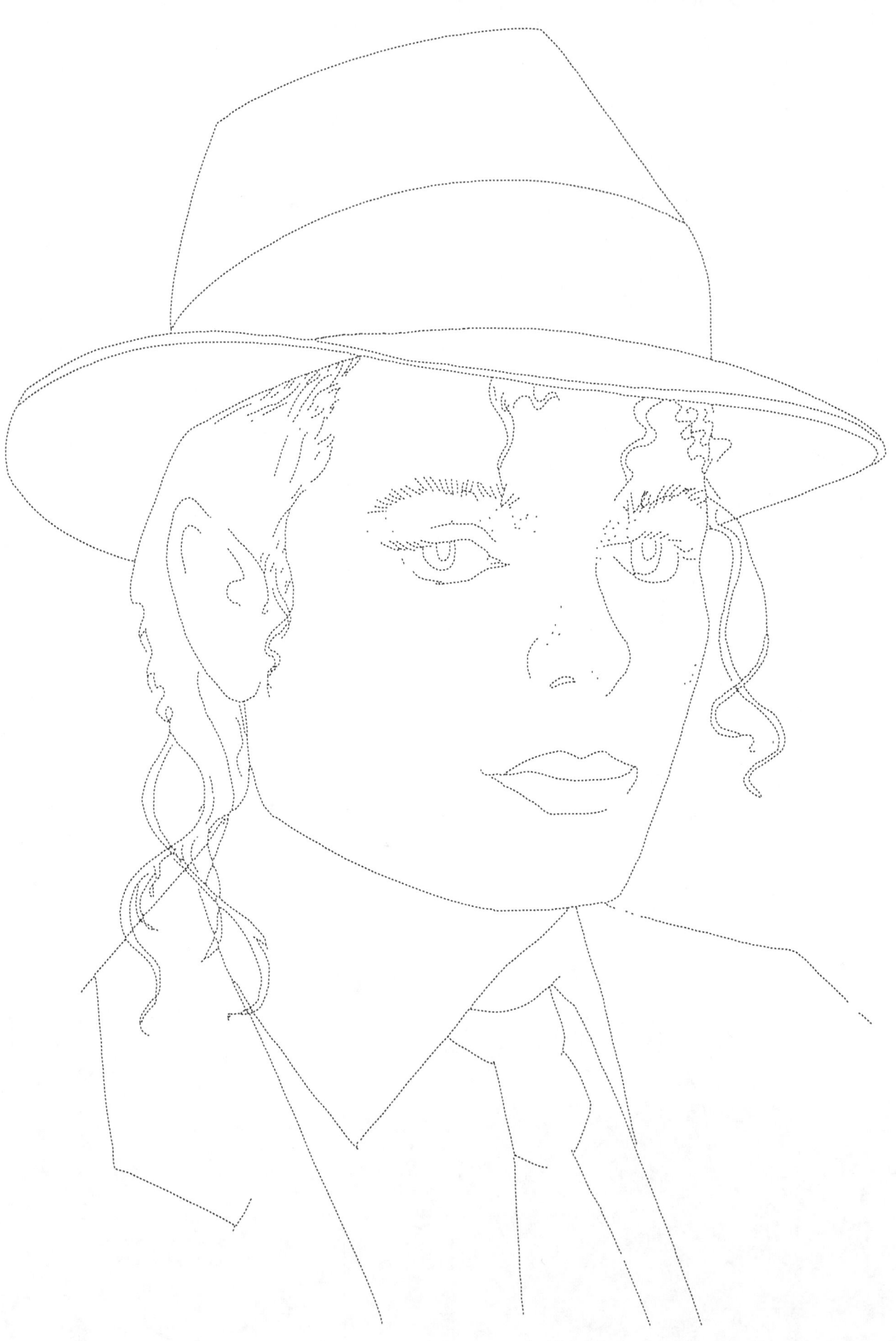

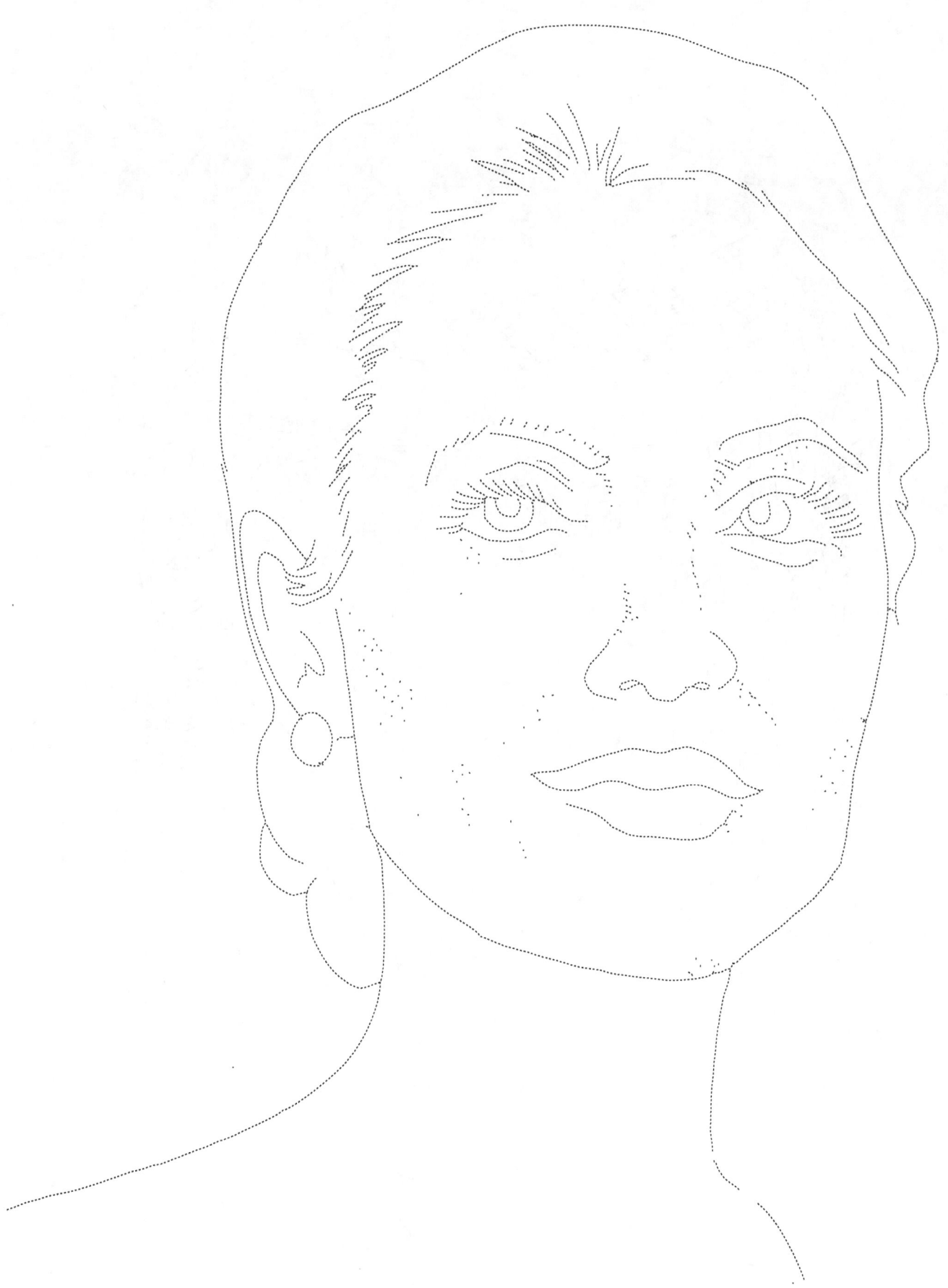

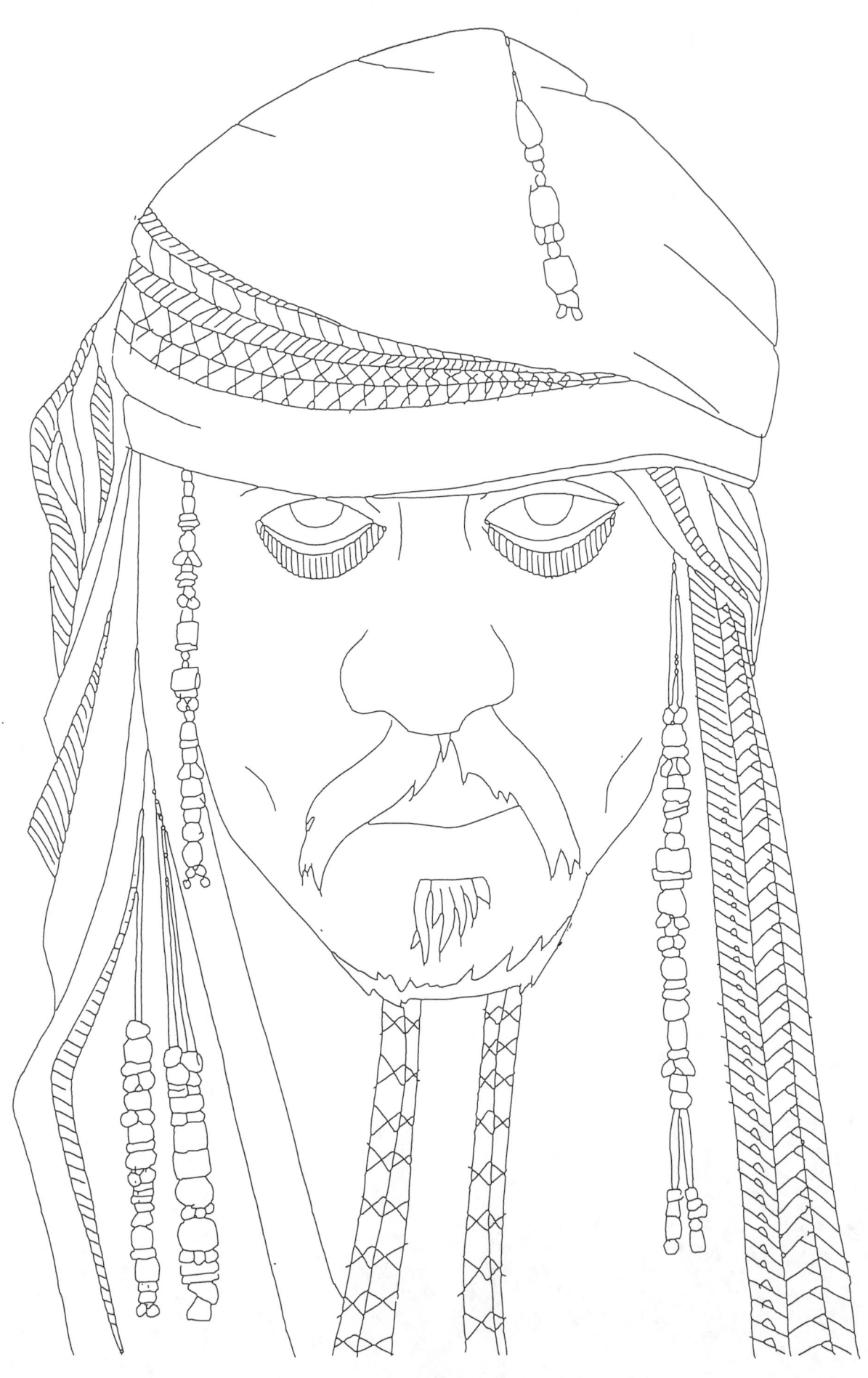

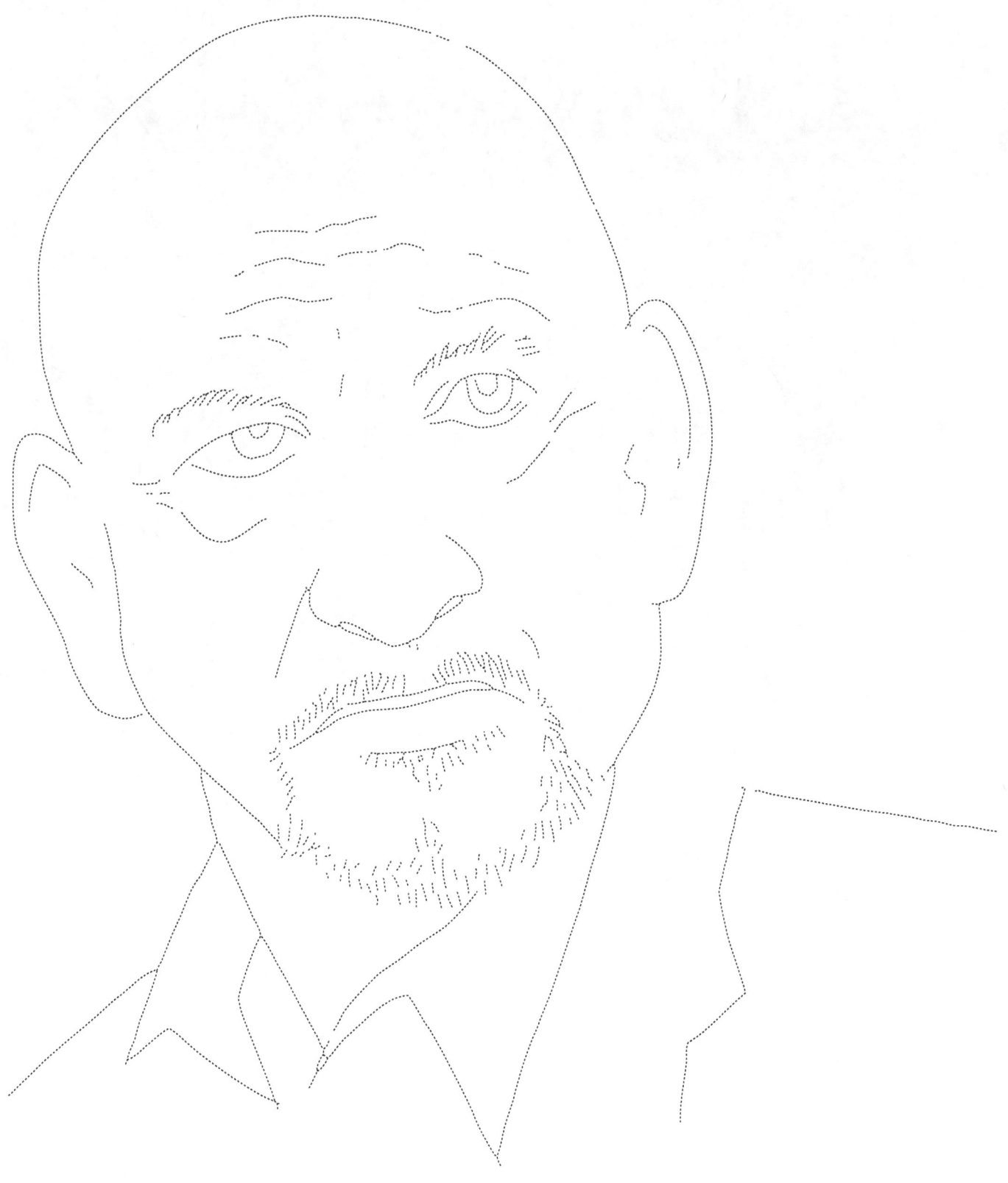

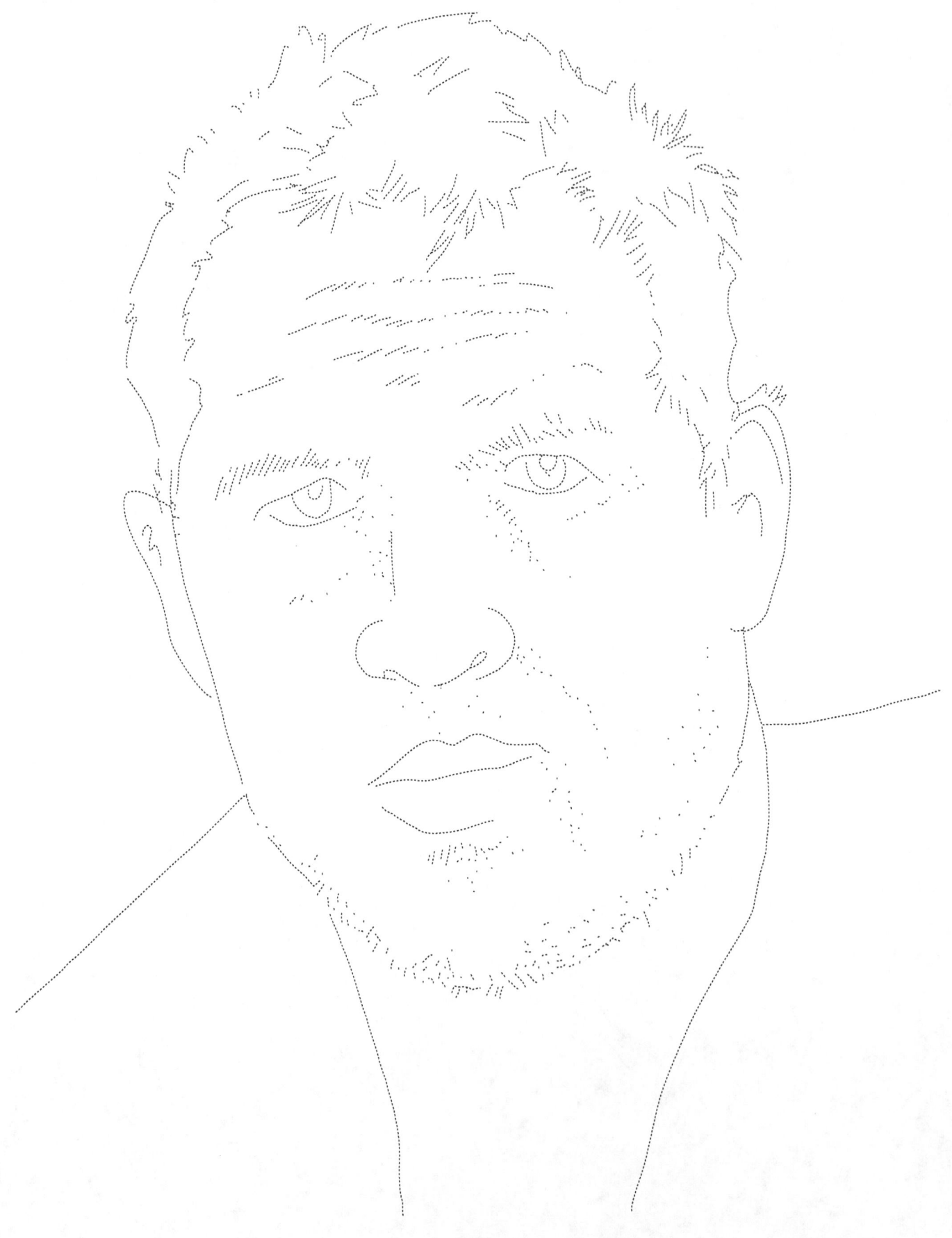

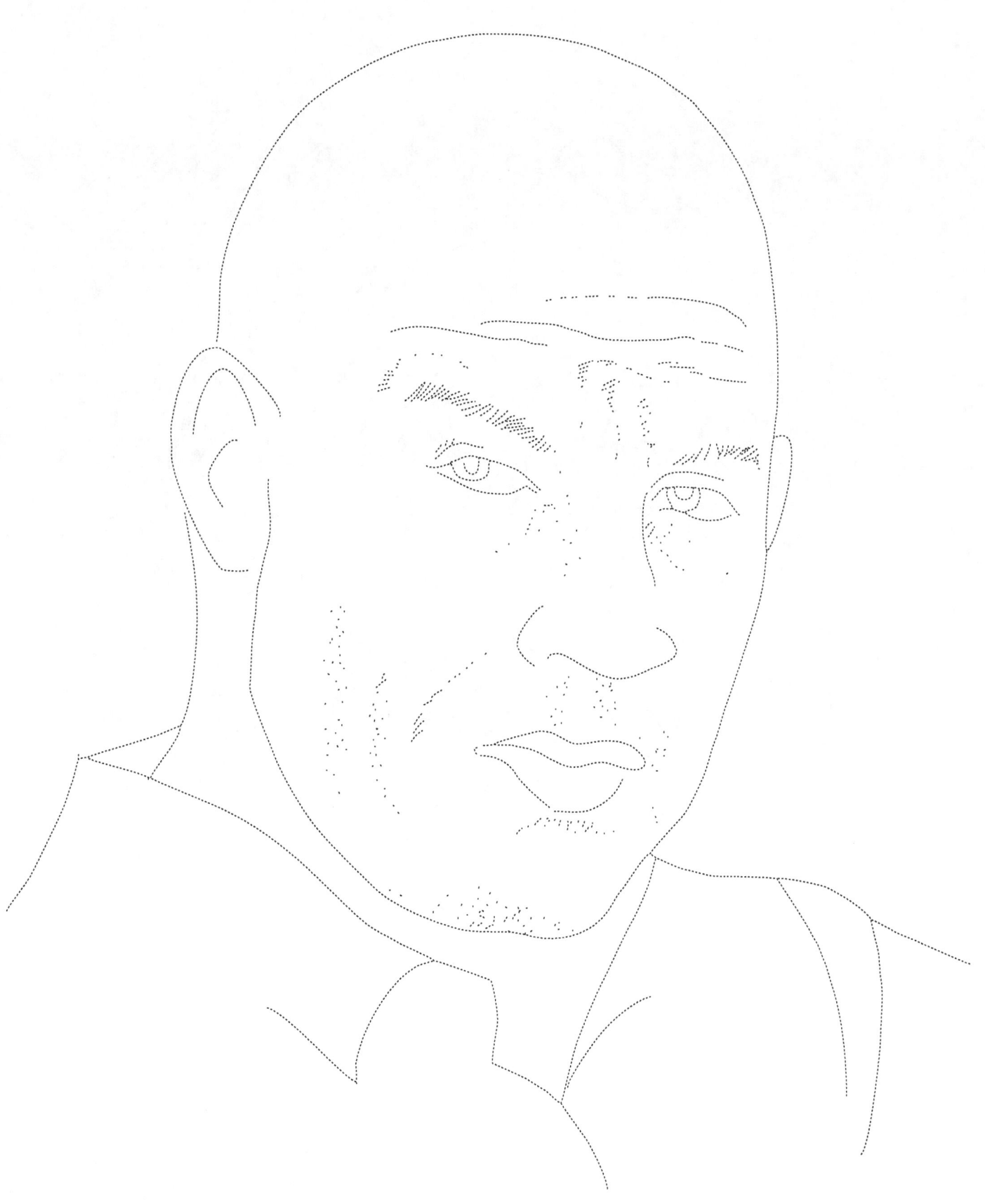

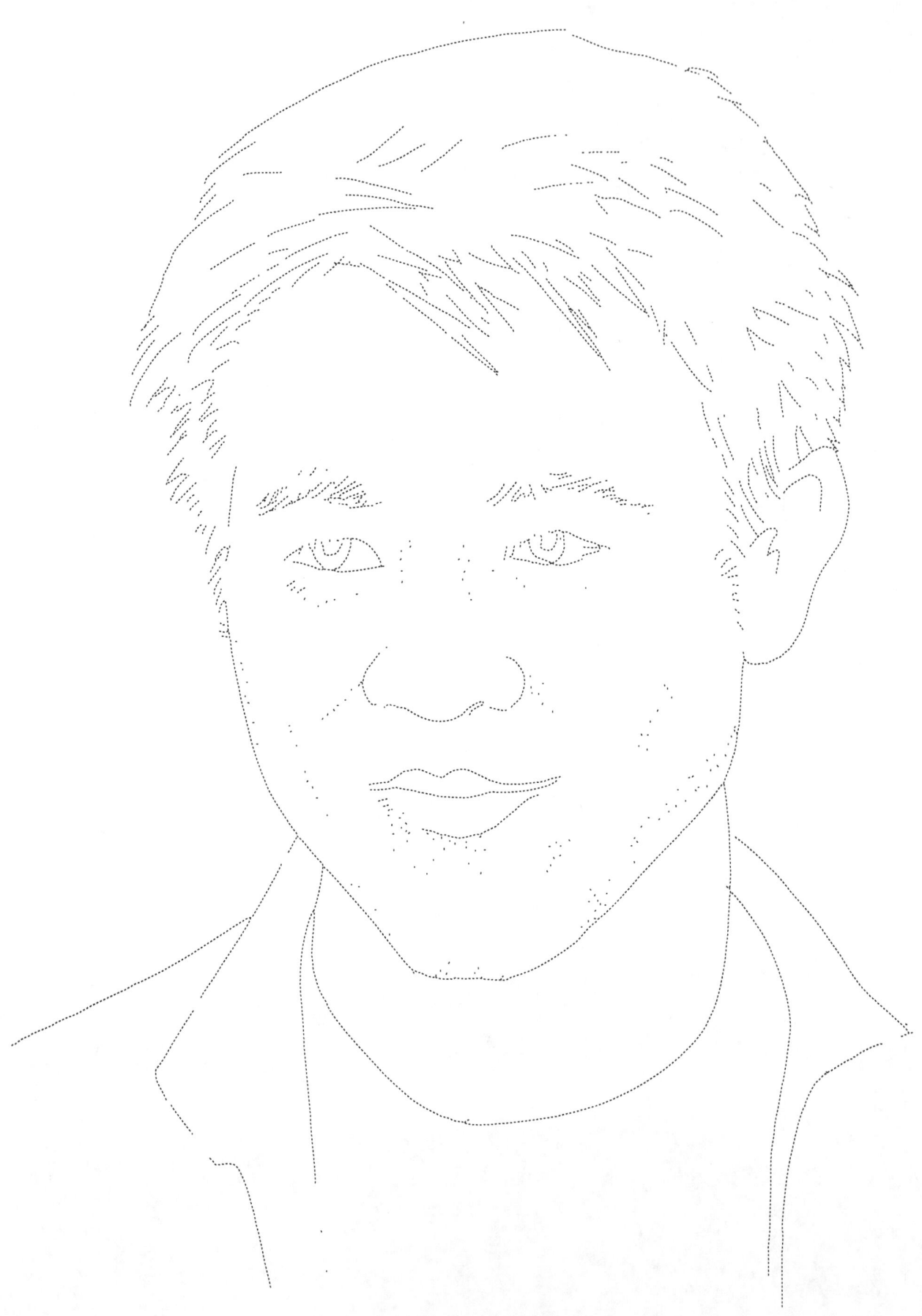

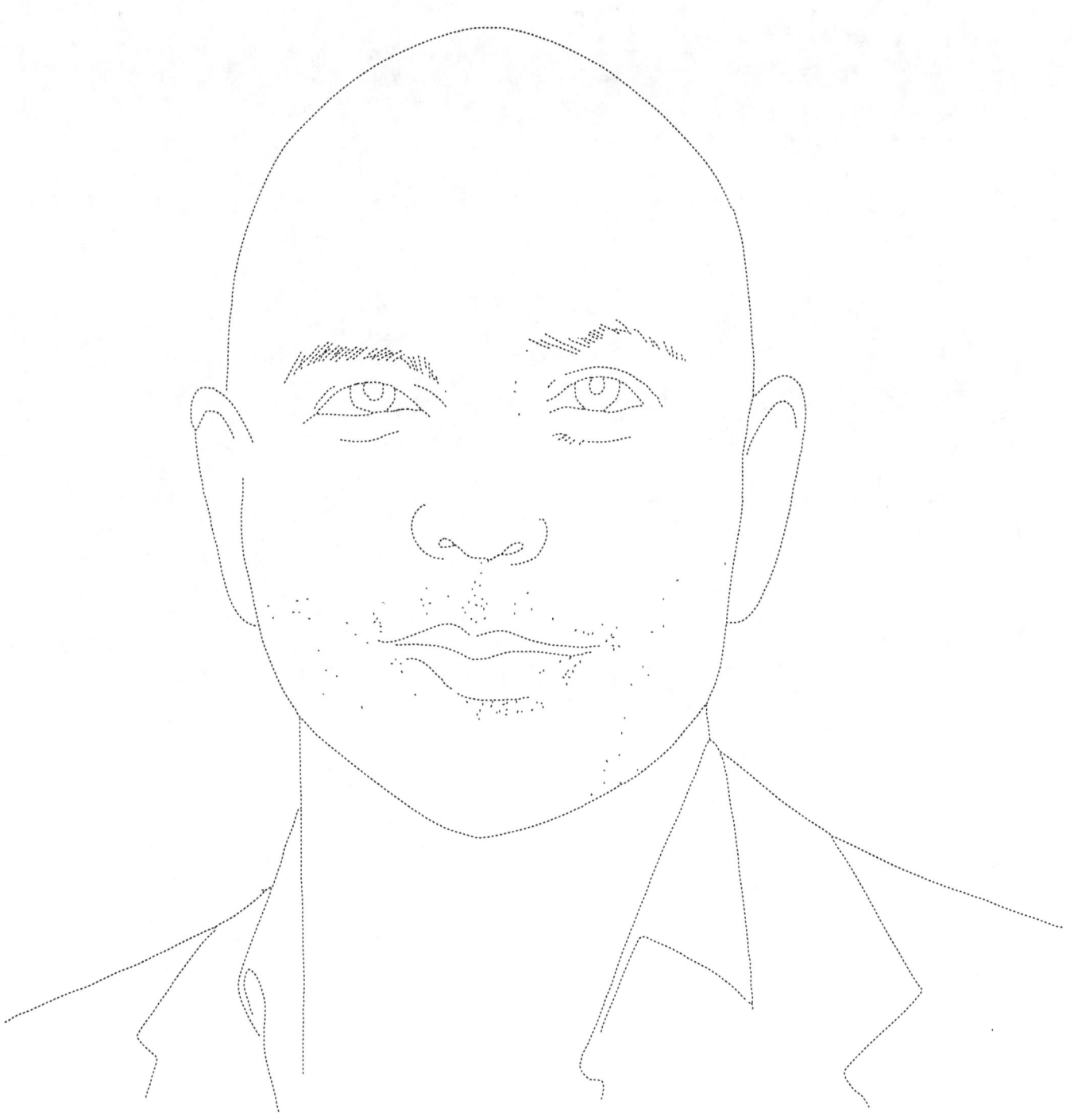

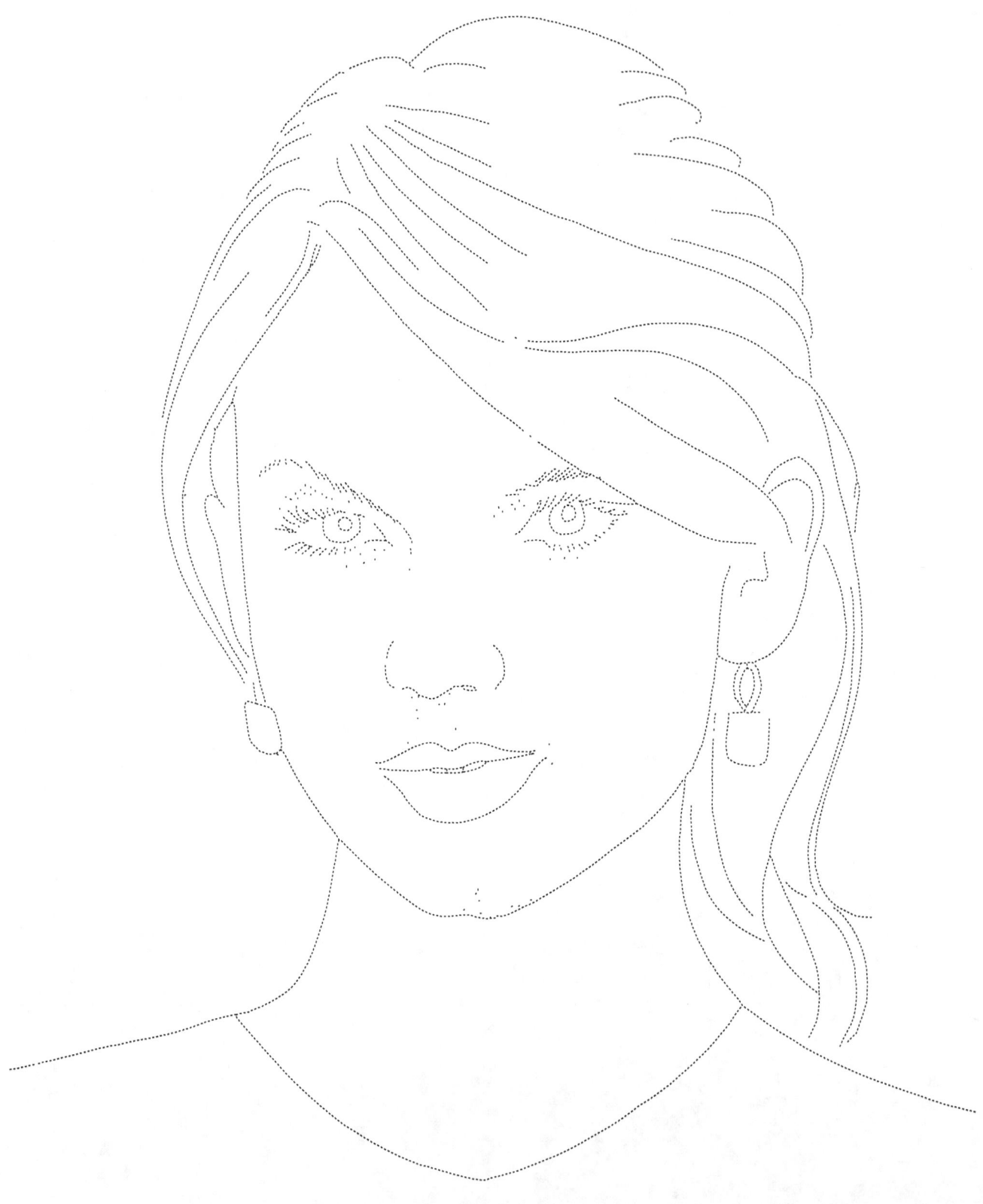

14

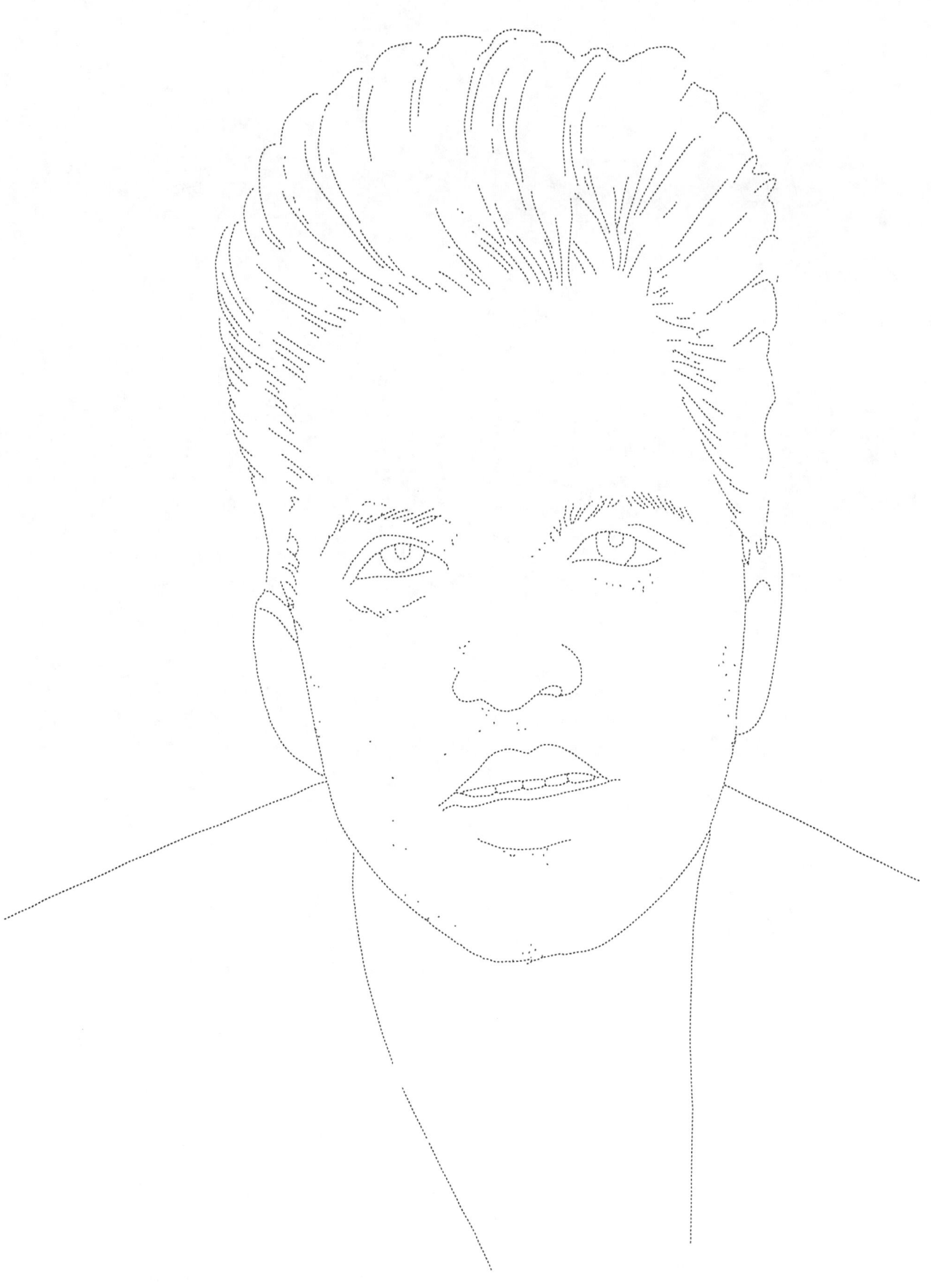

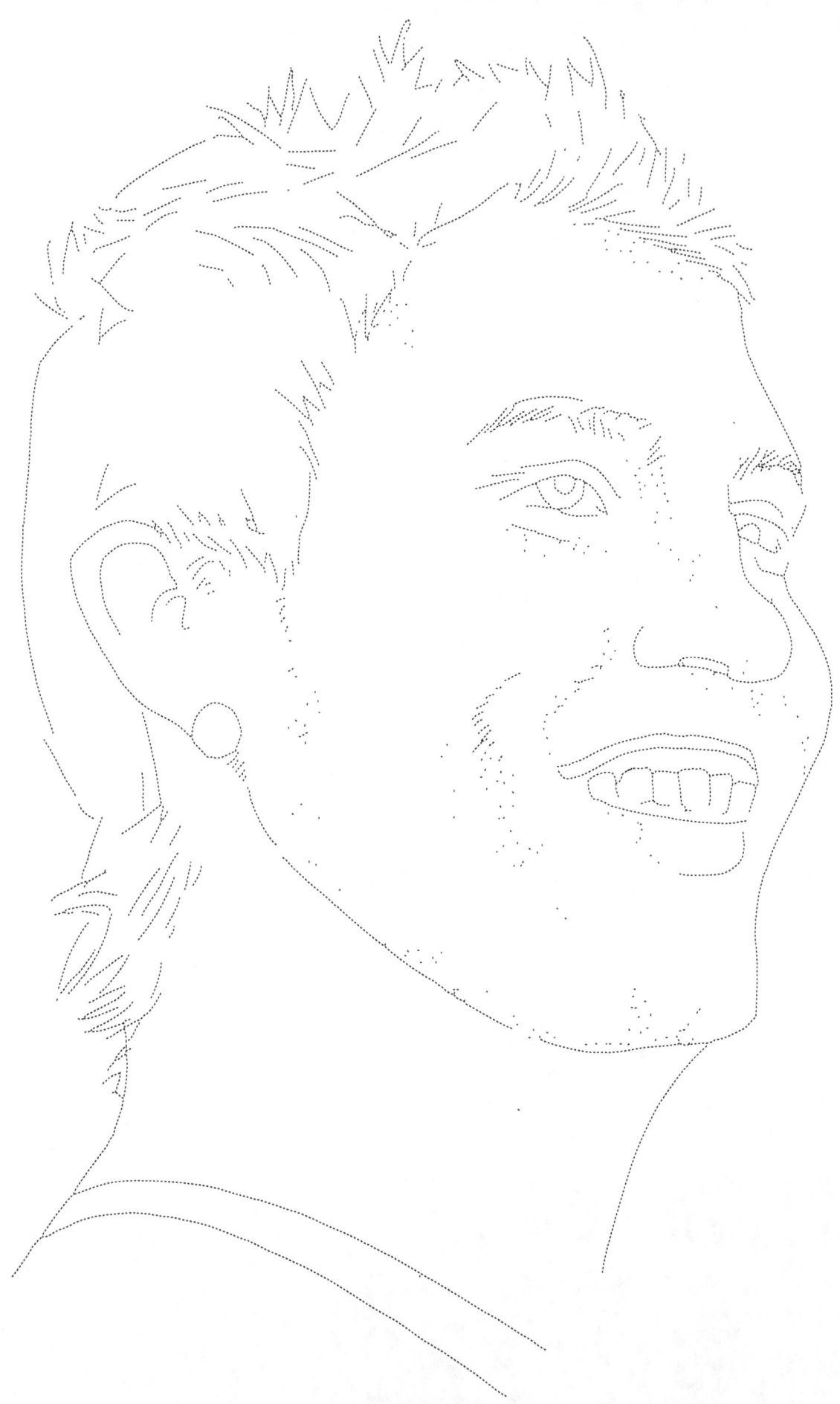

16

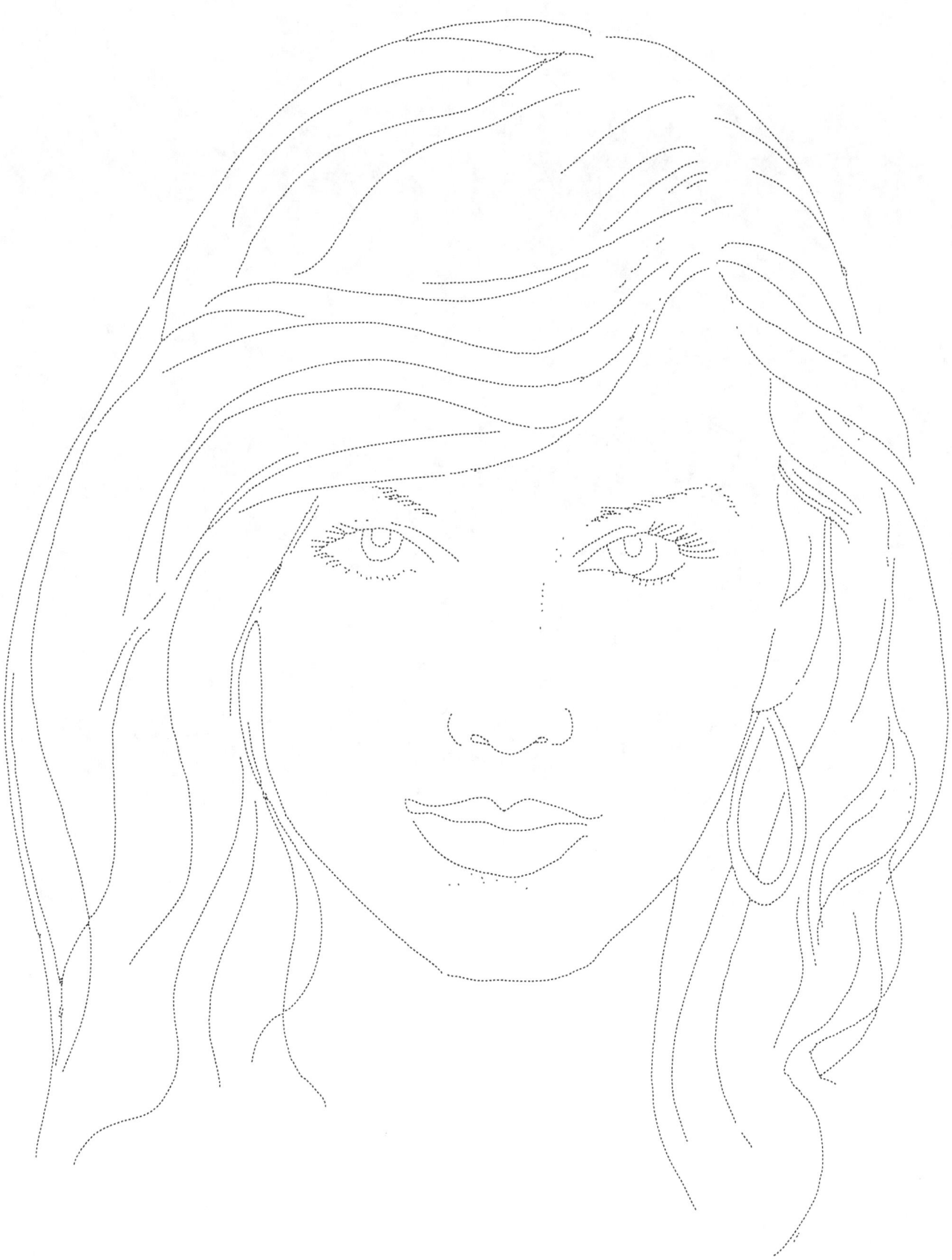

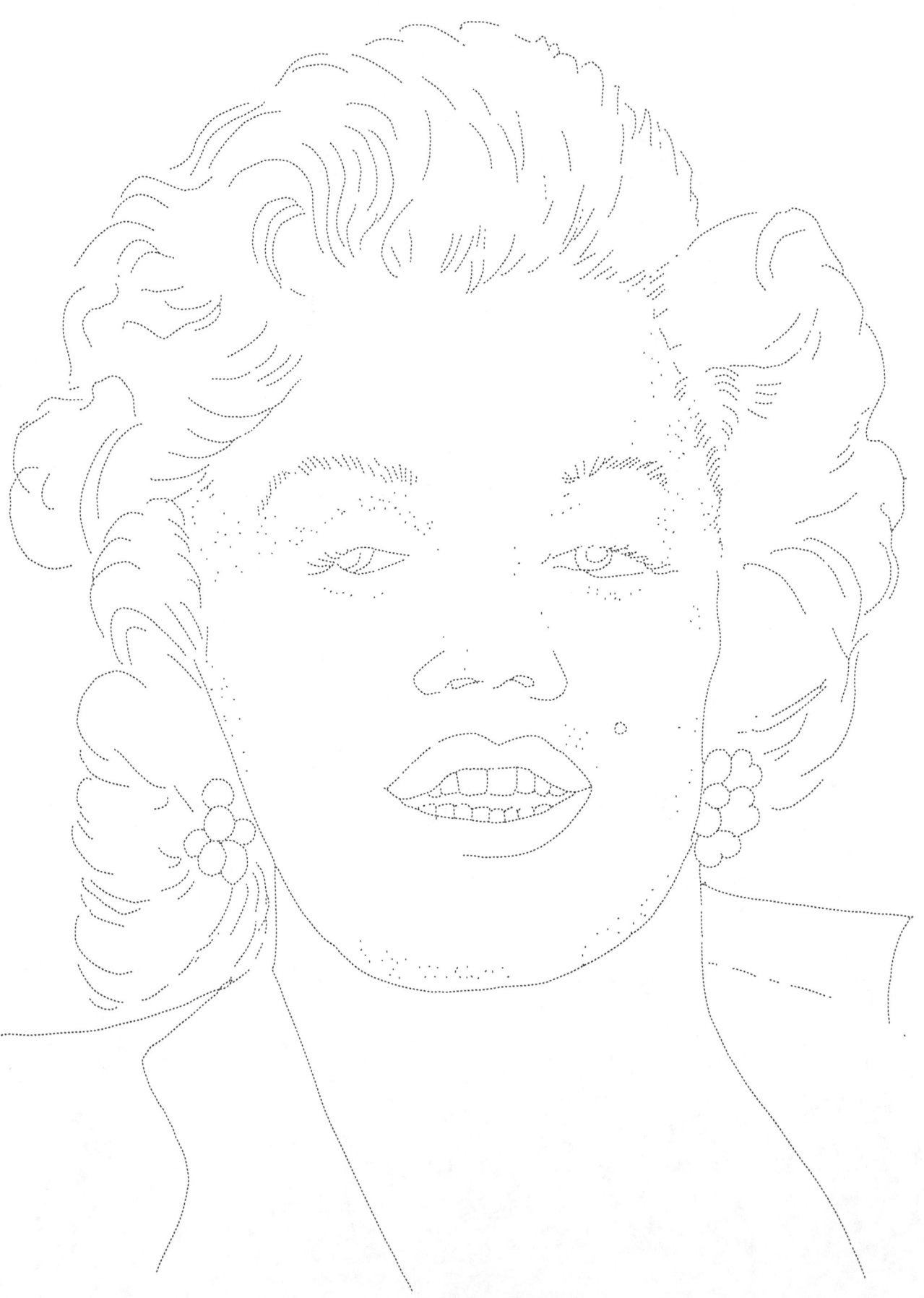

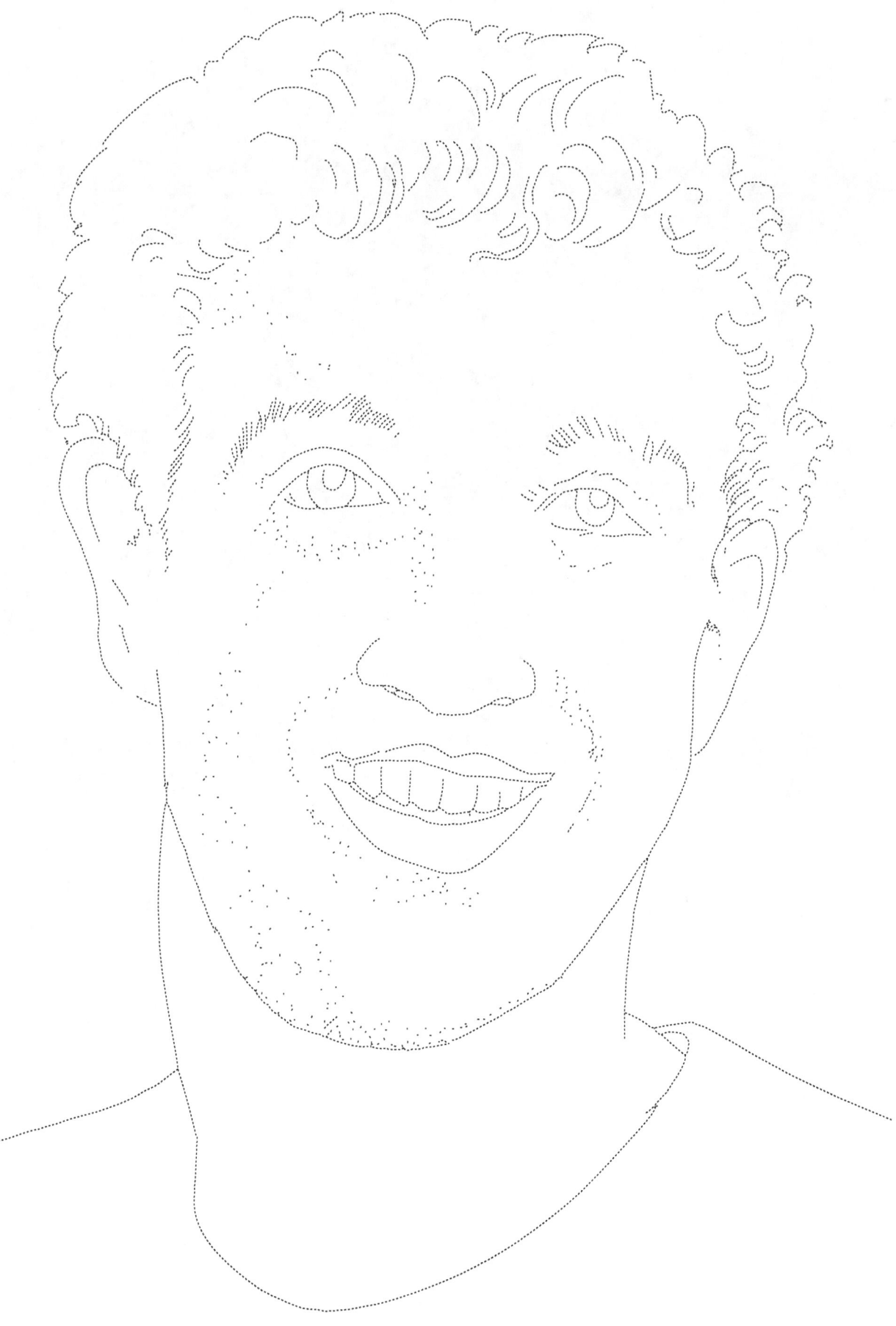

19

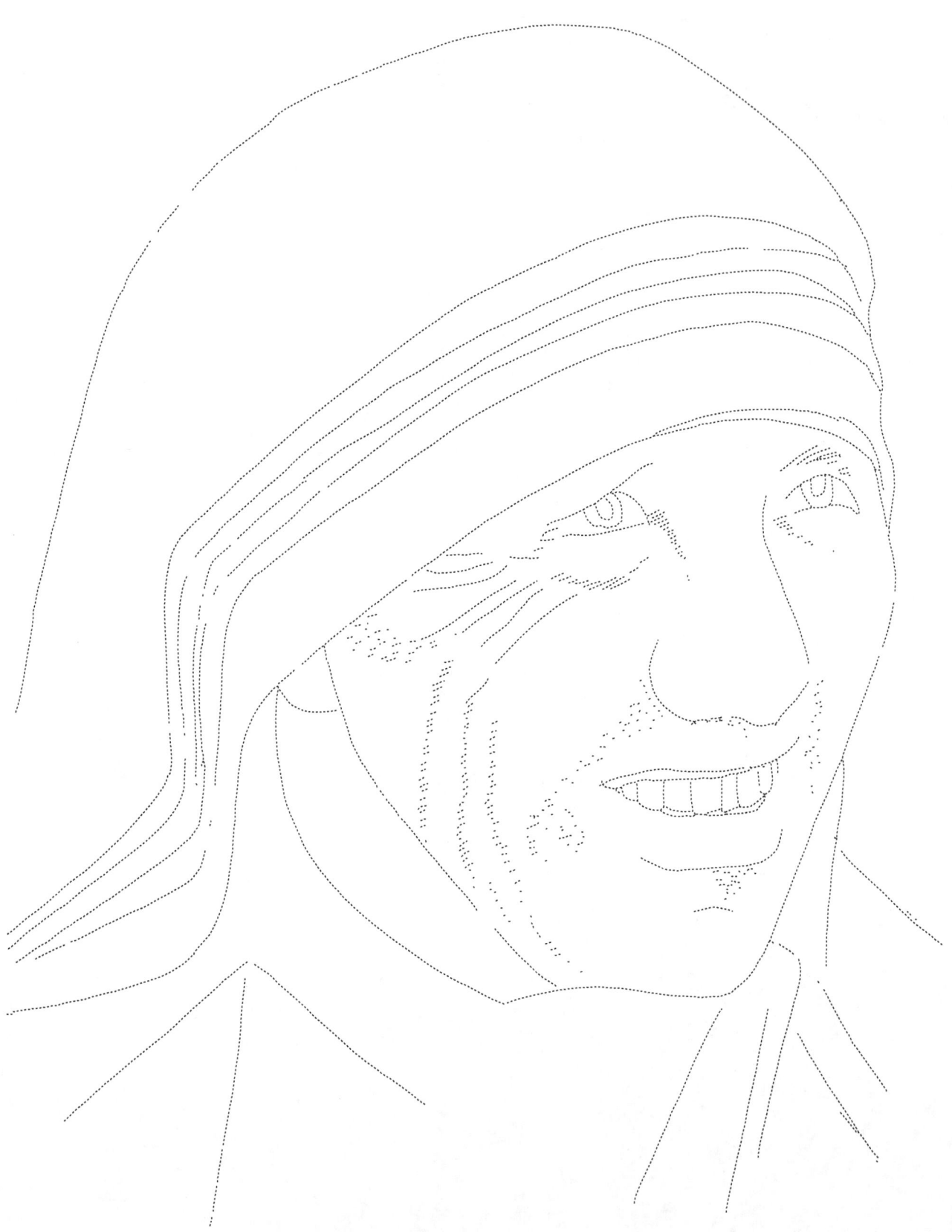

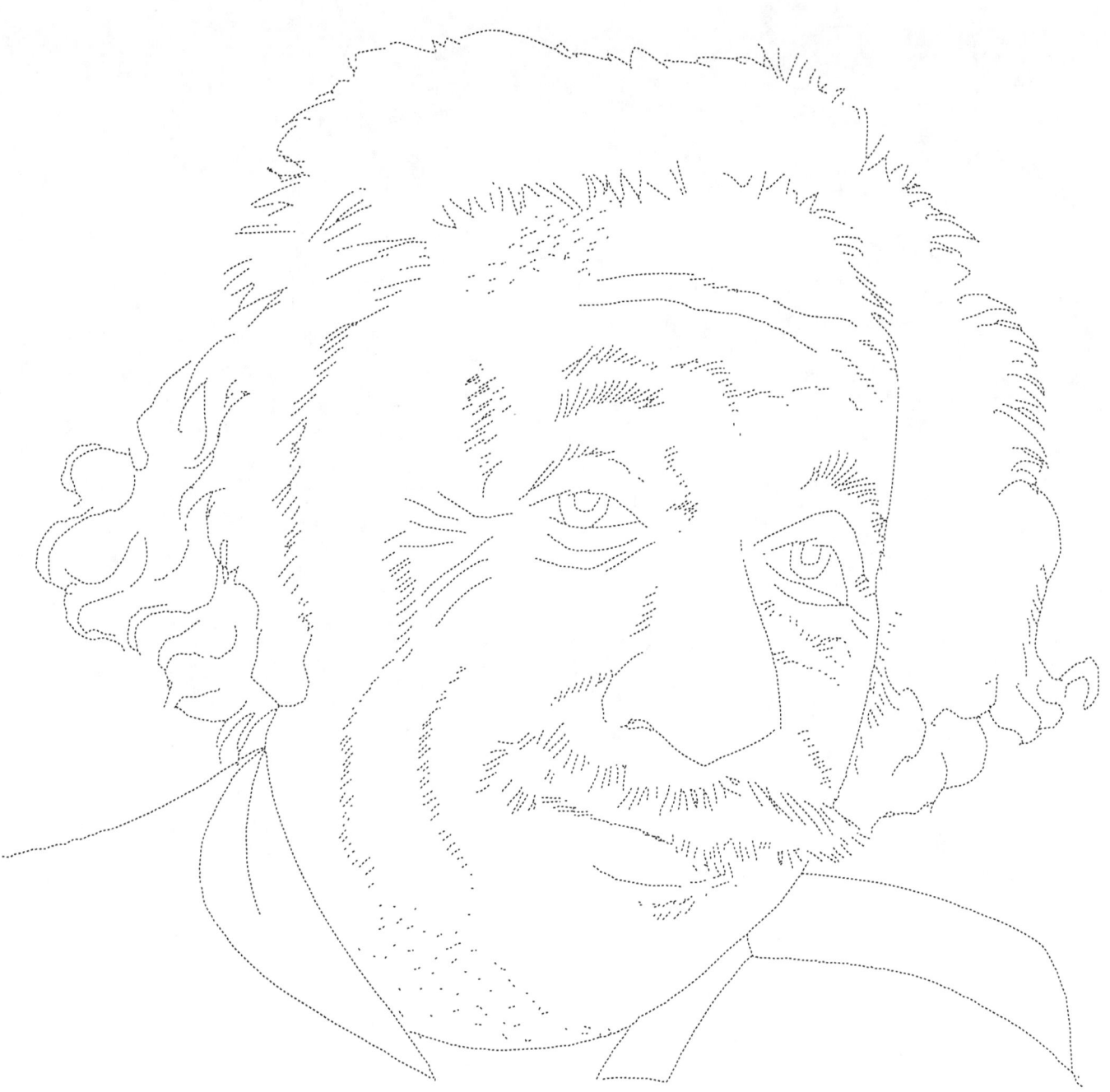

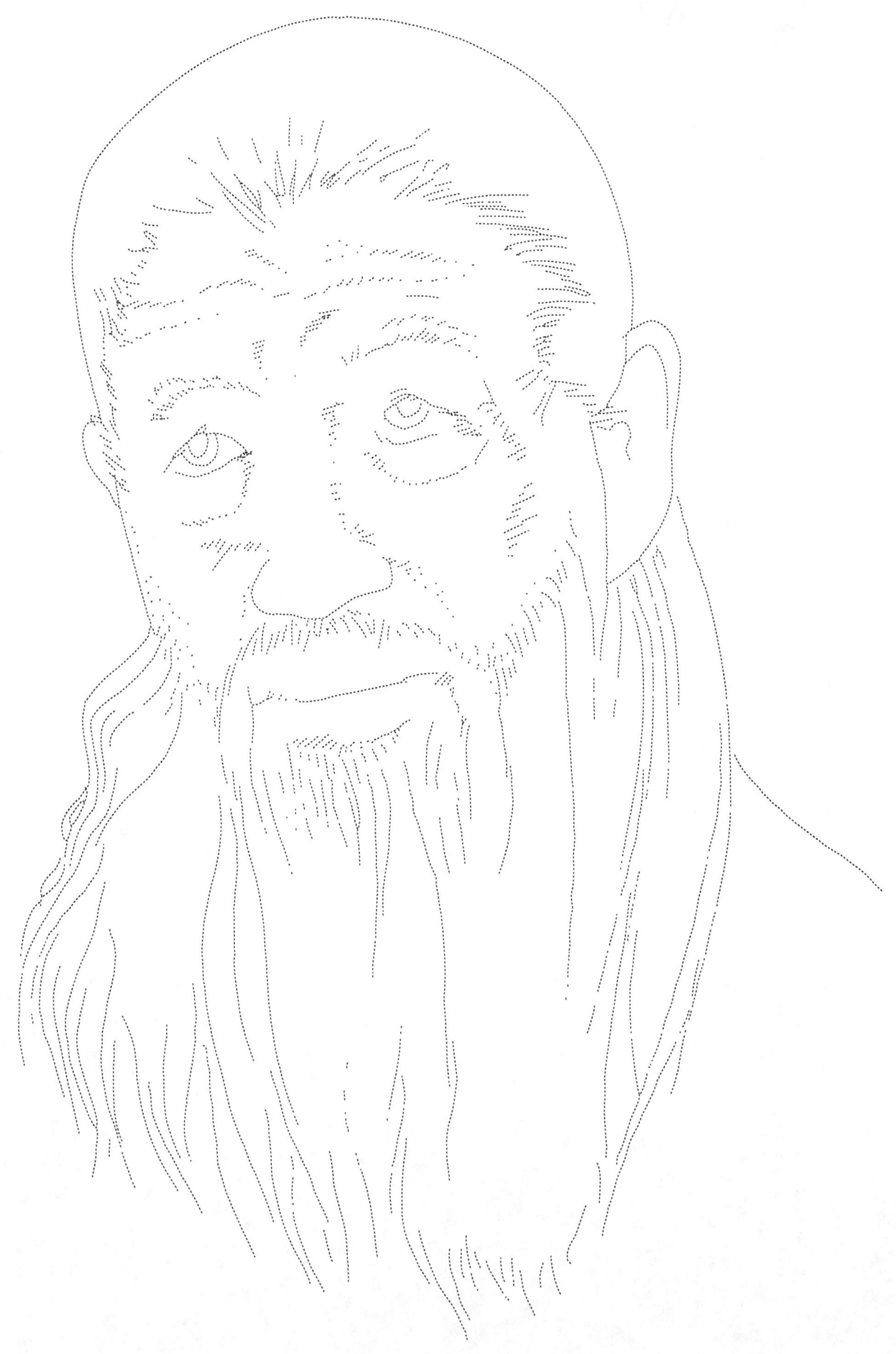

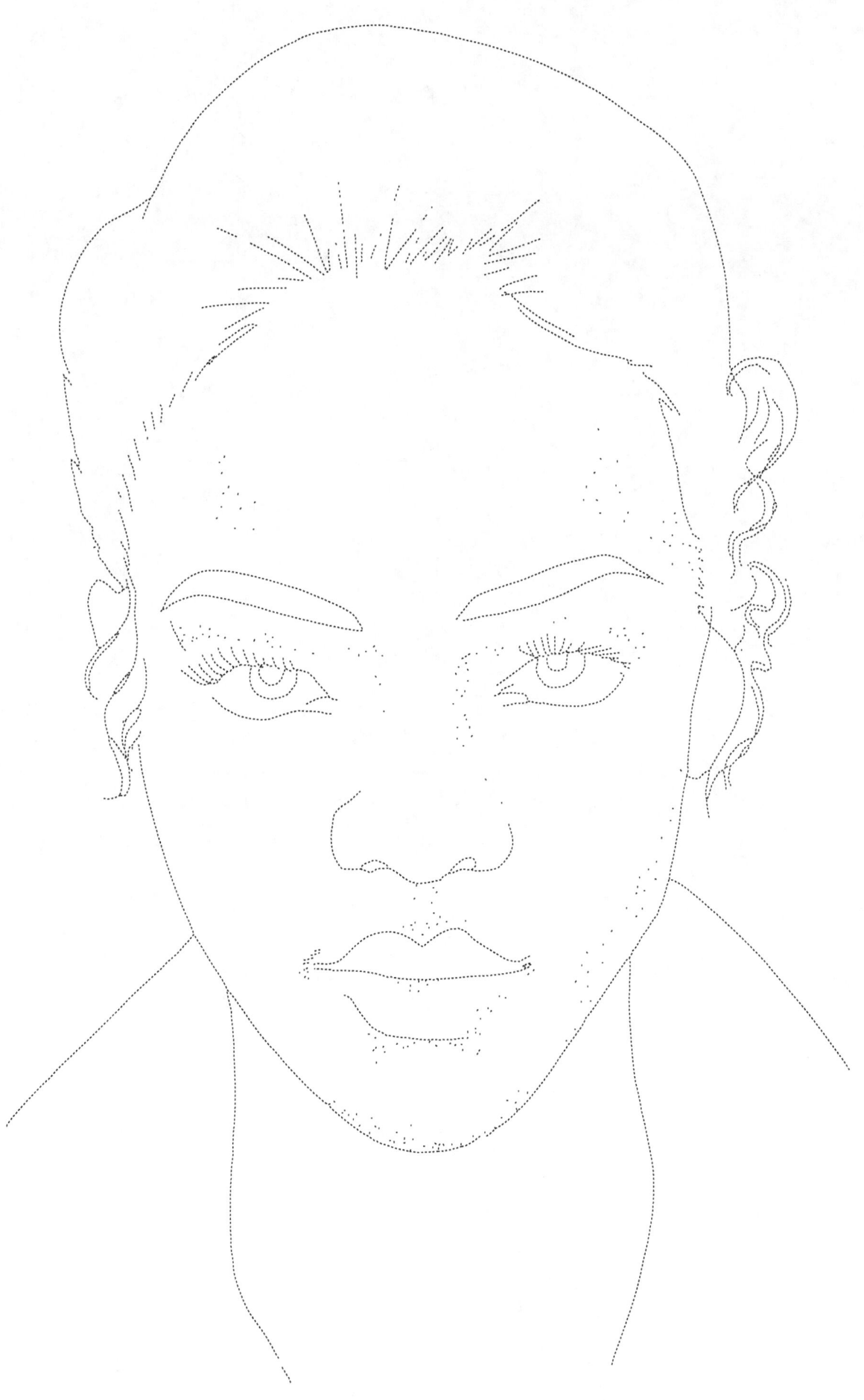

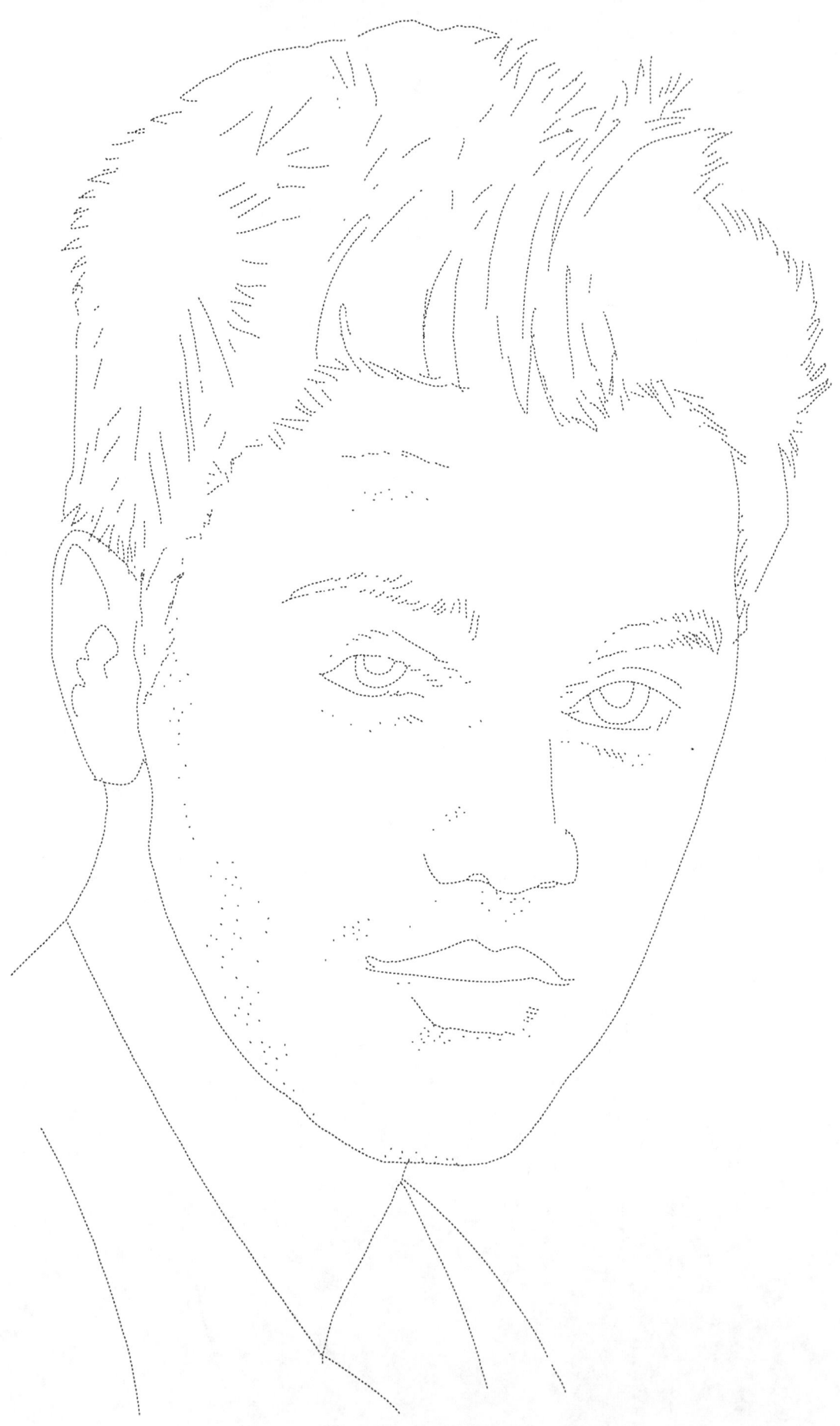

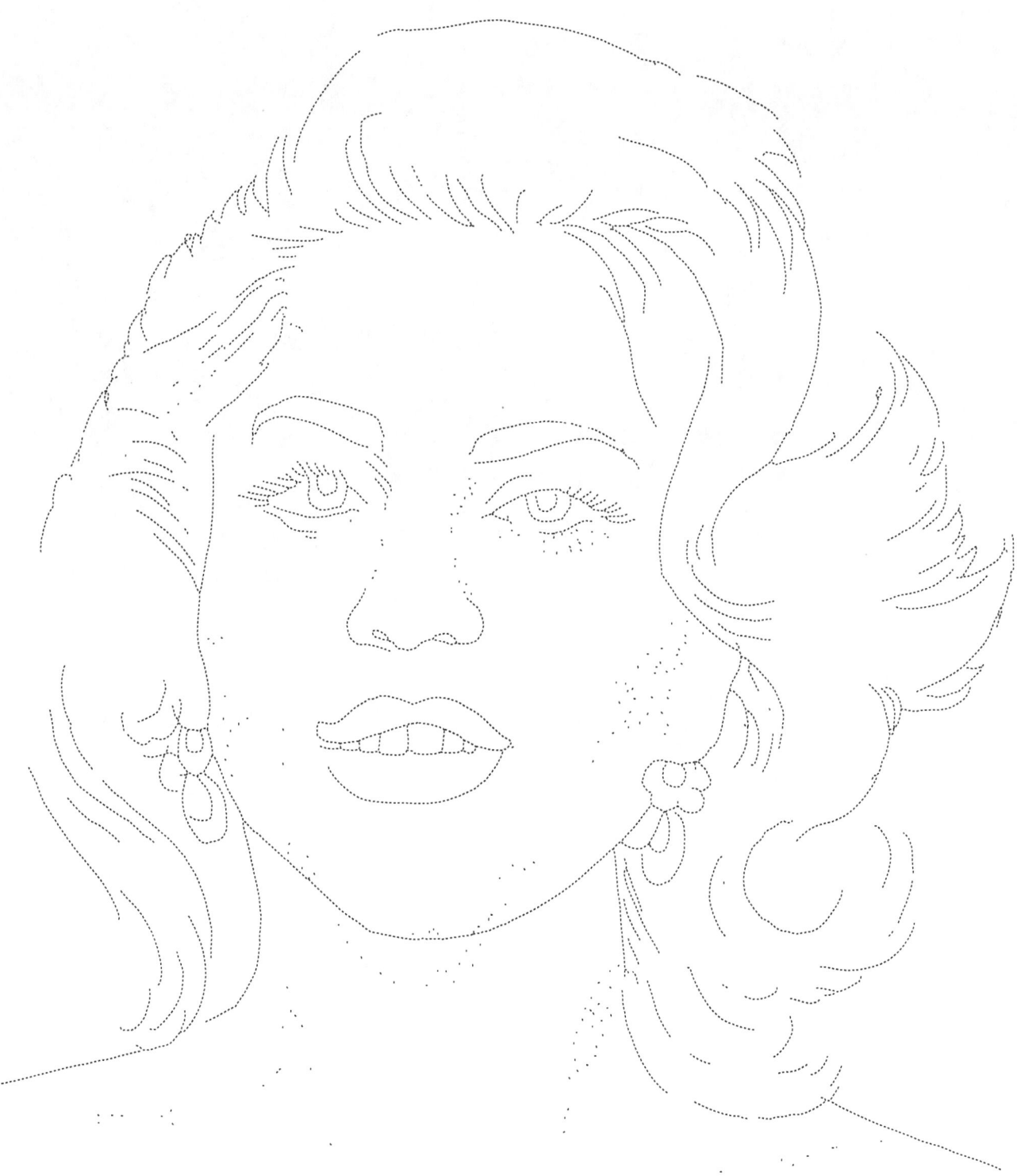

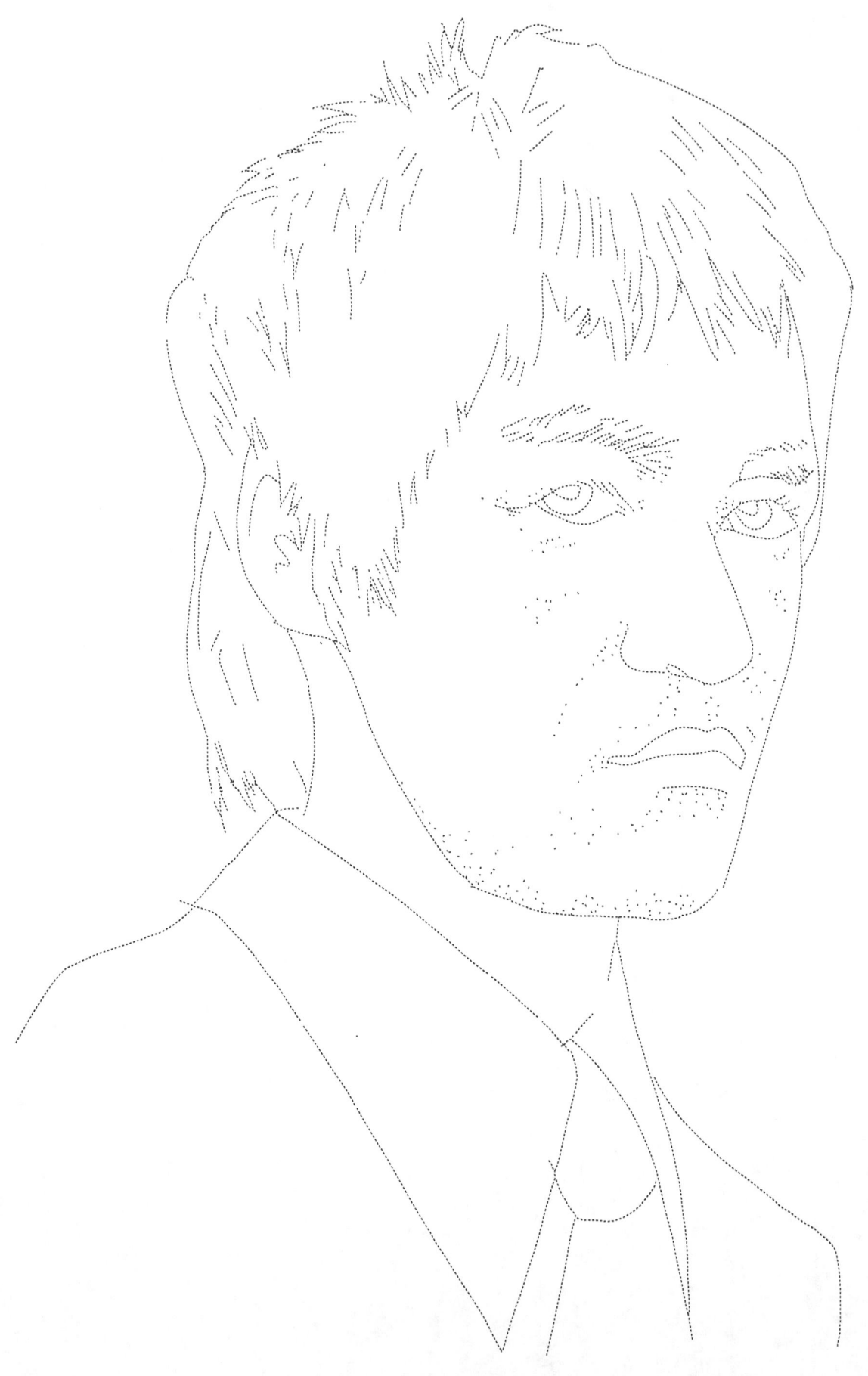

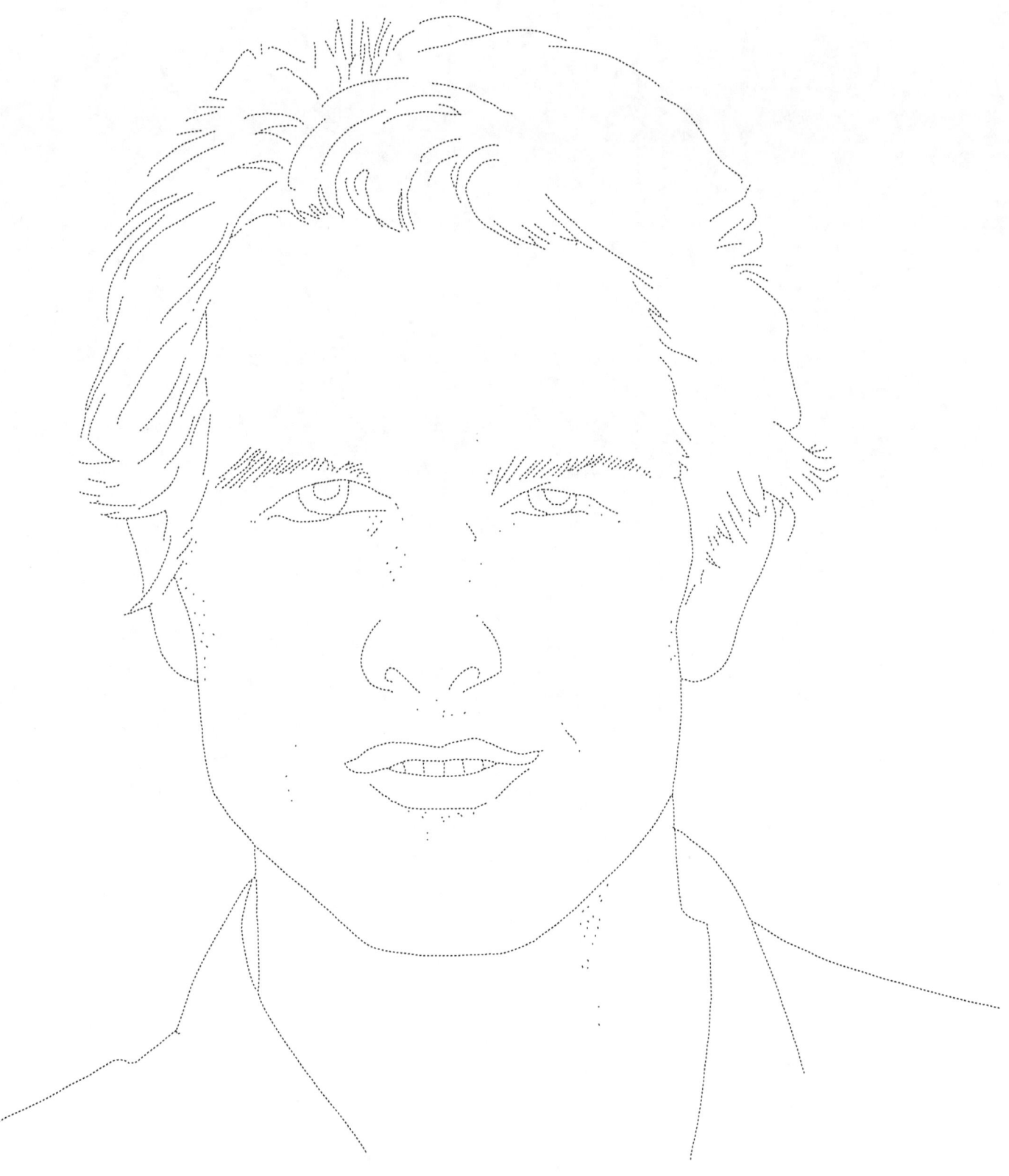

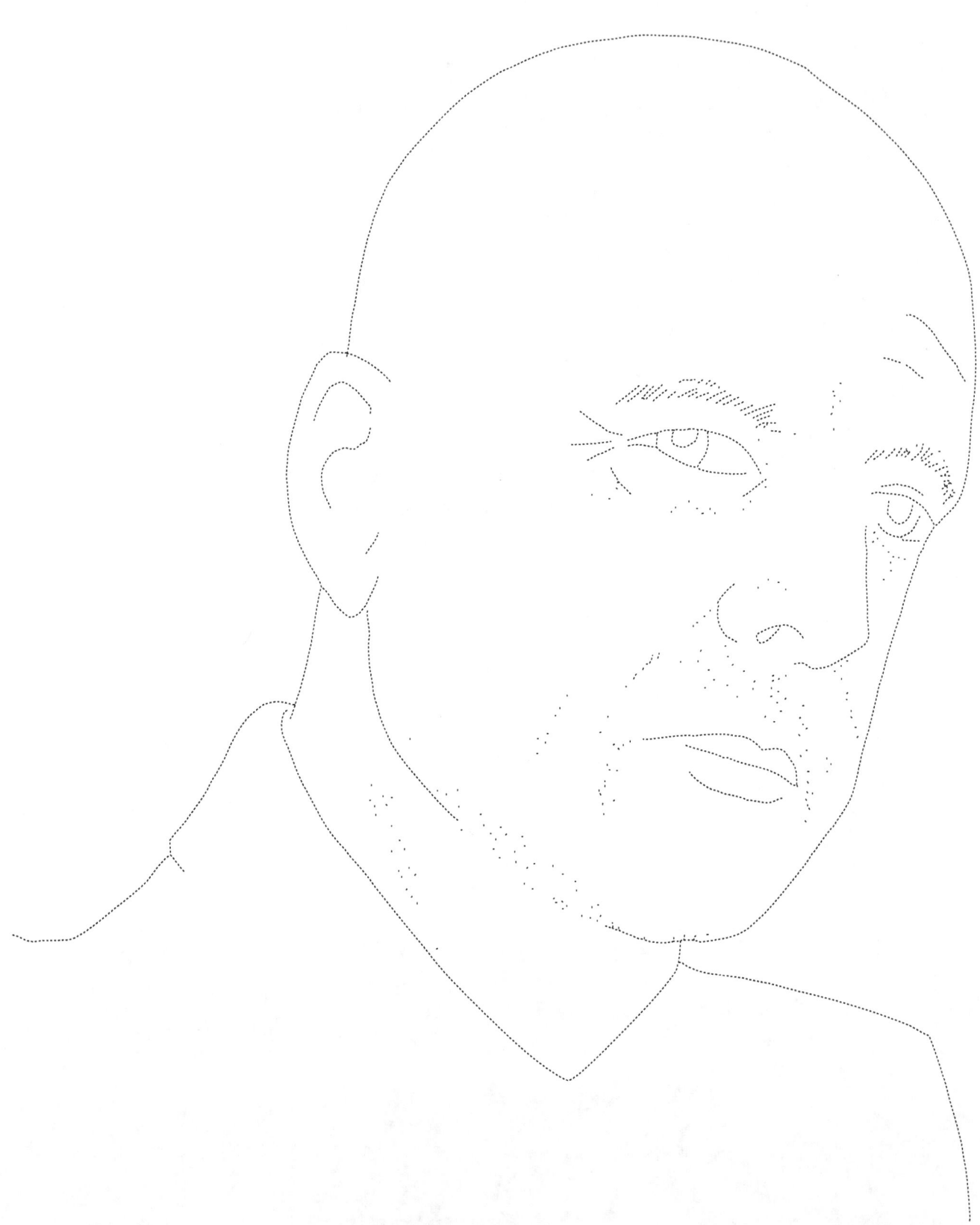

28

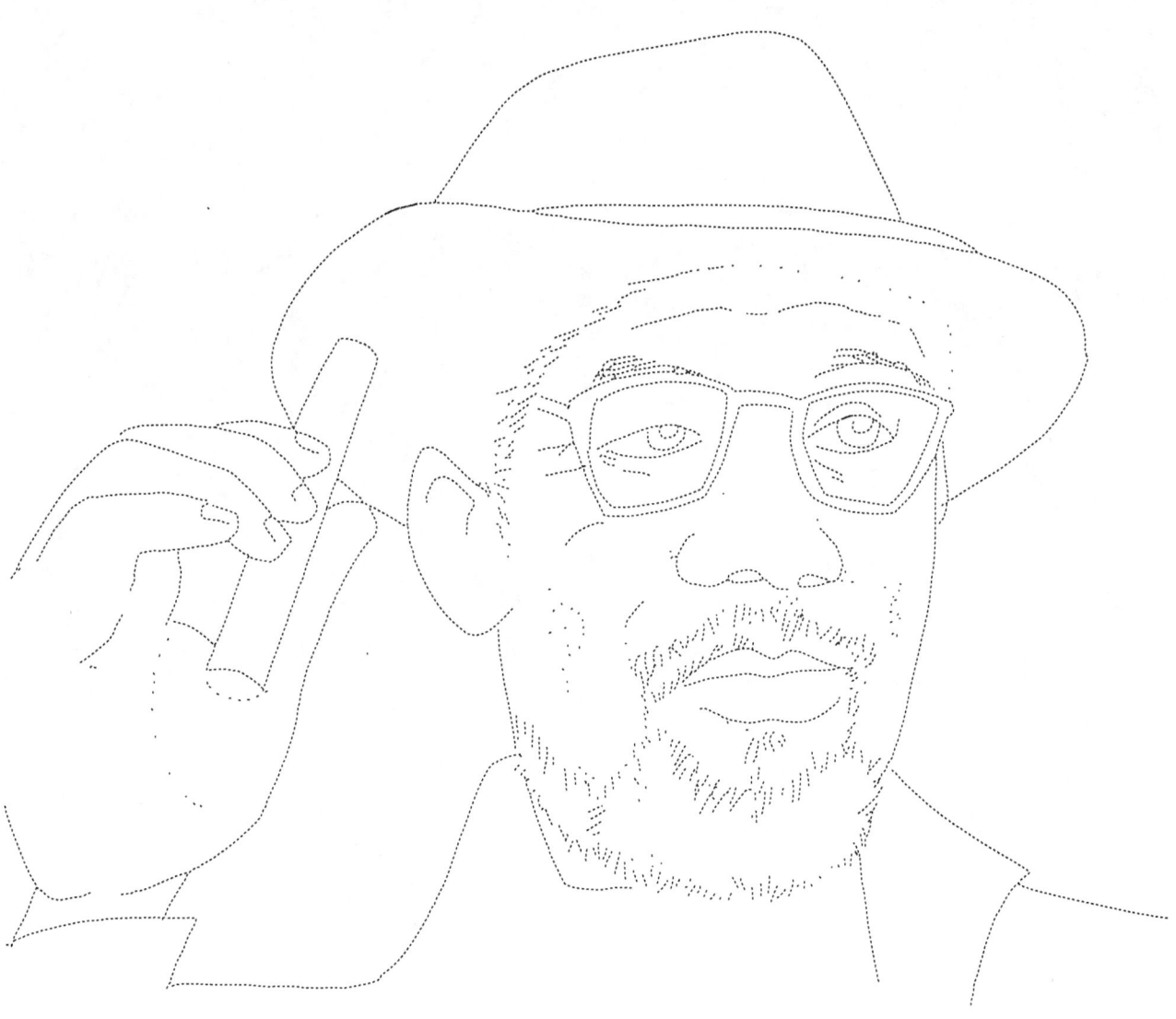

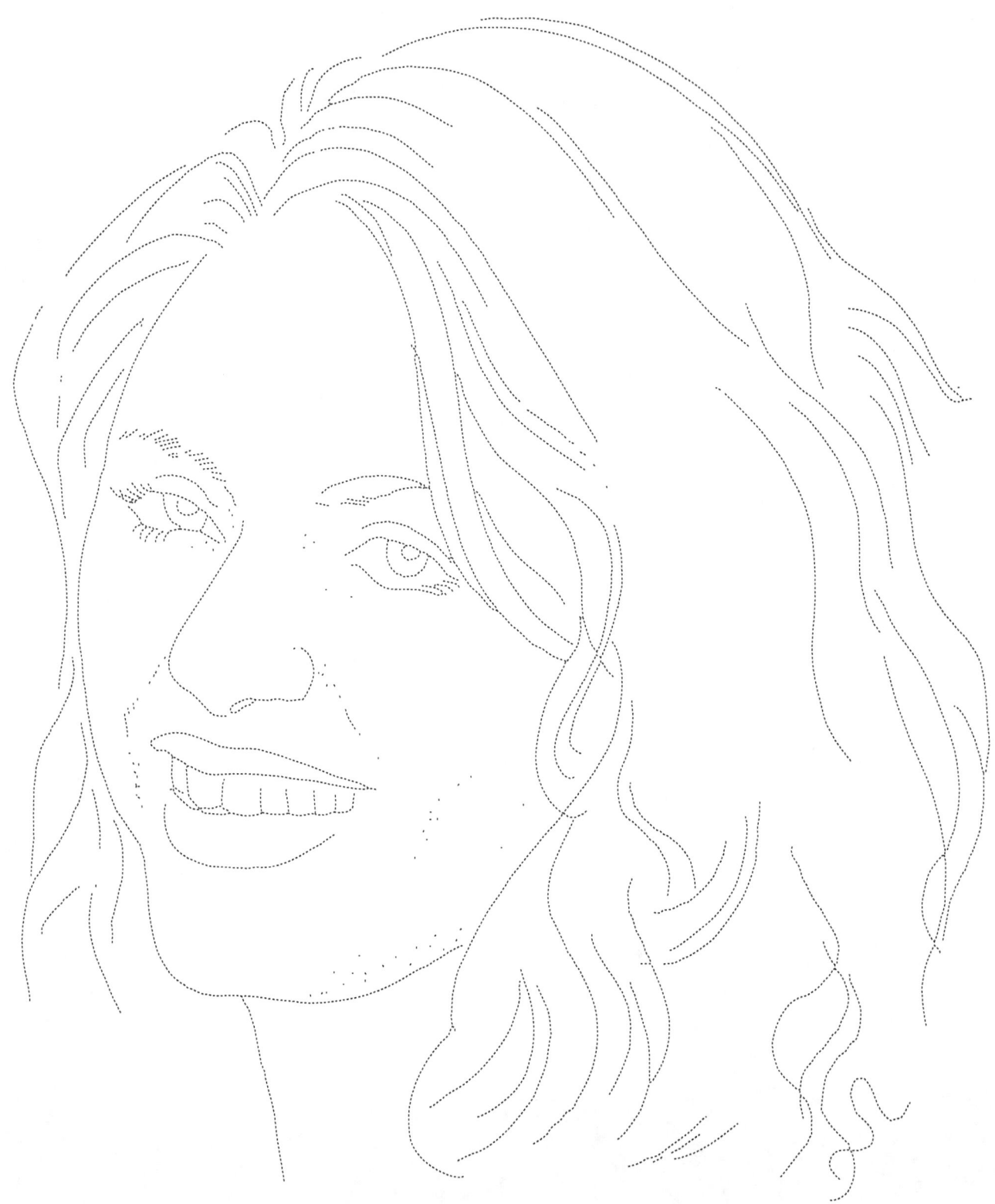

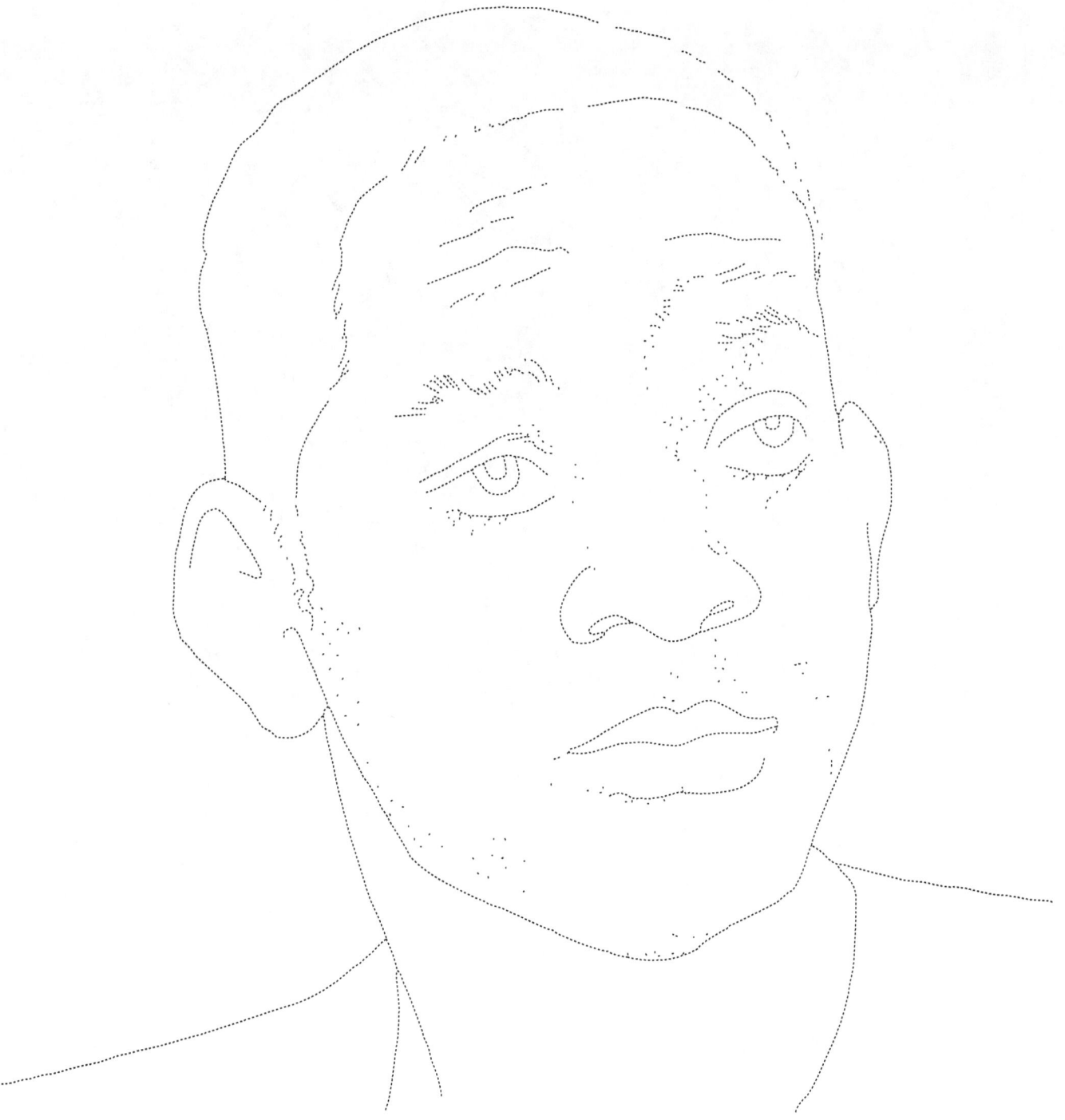

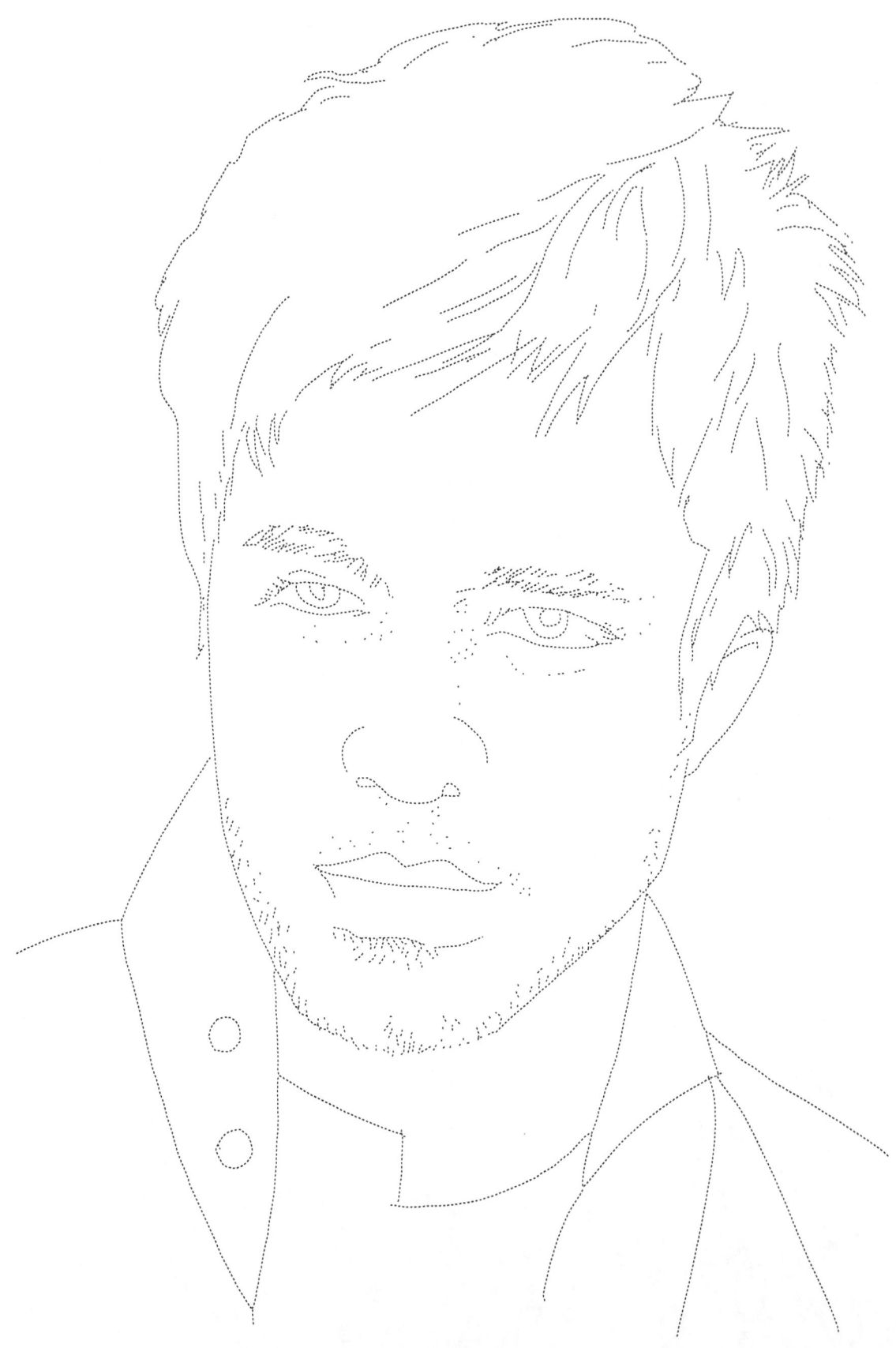

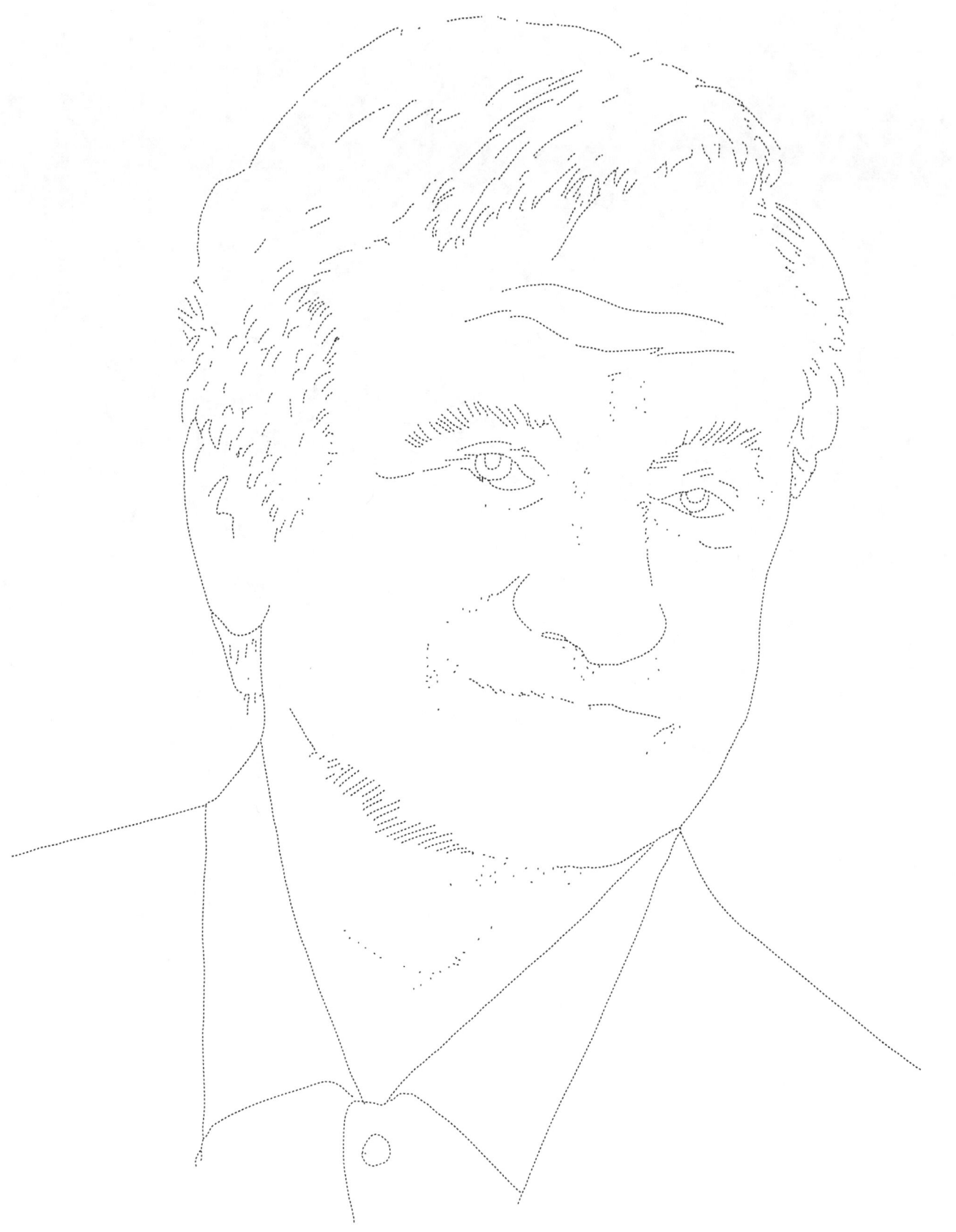

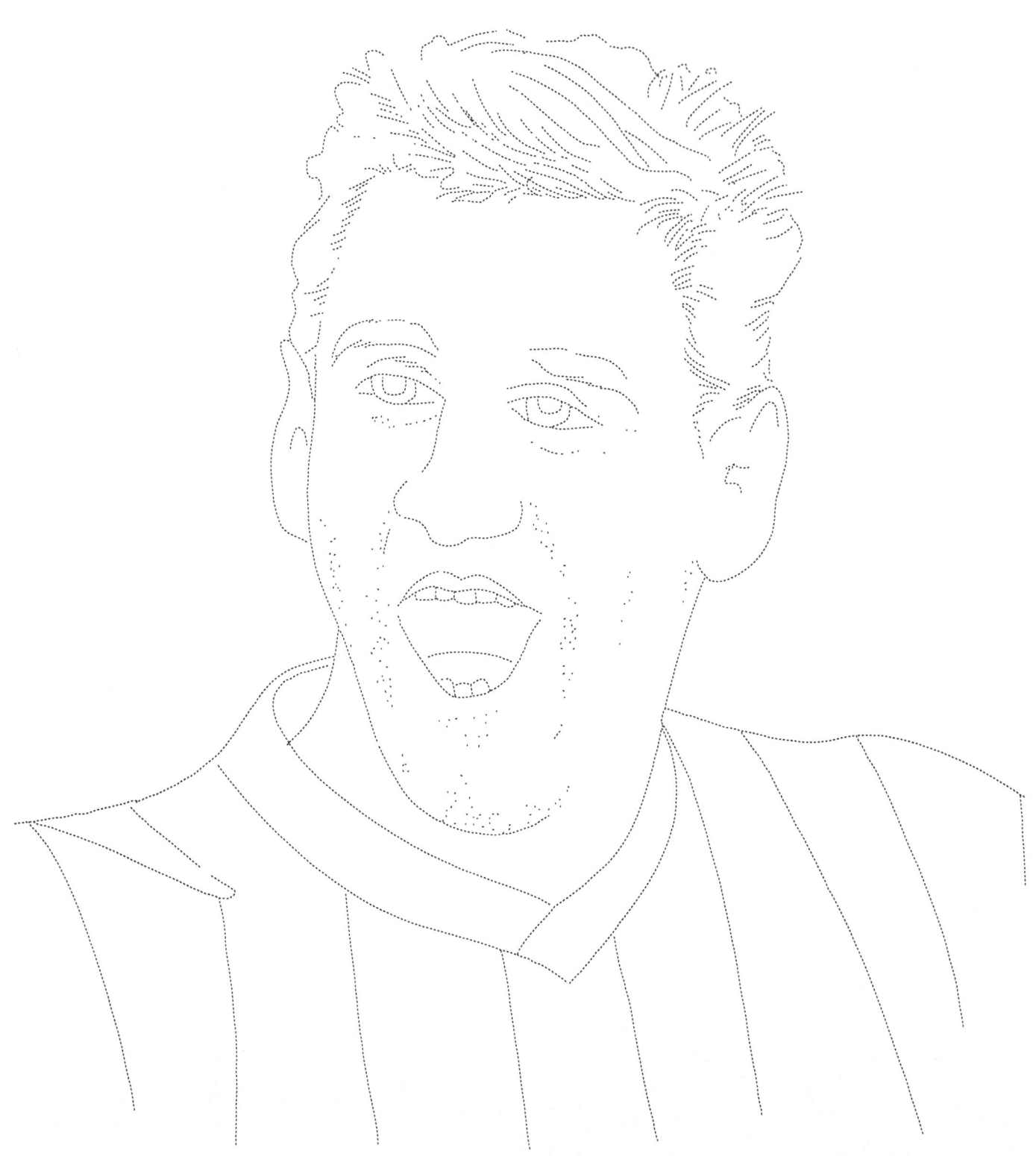

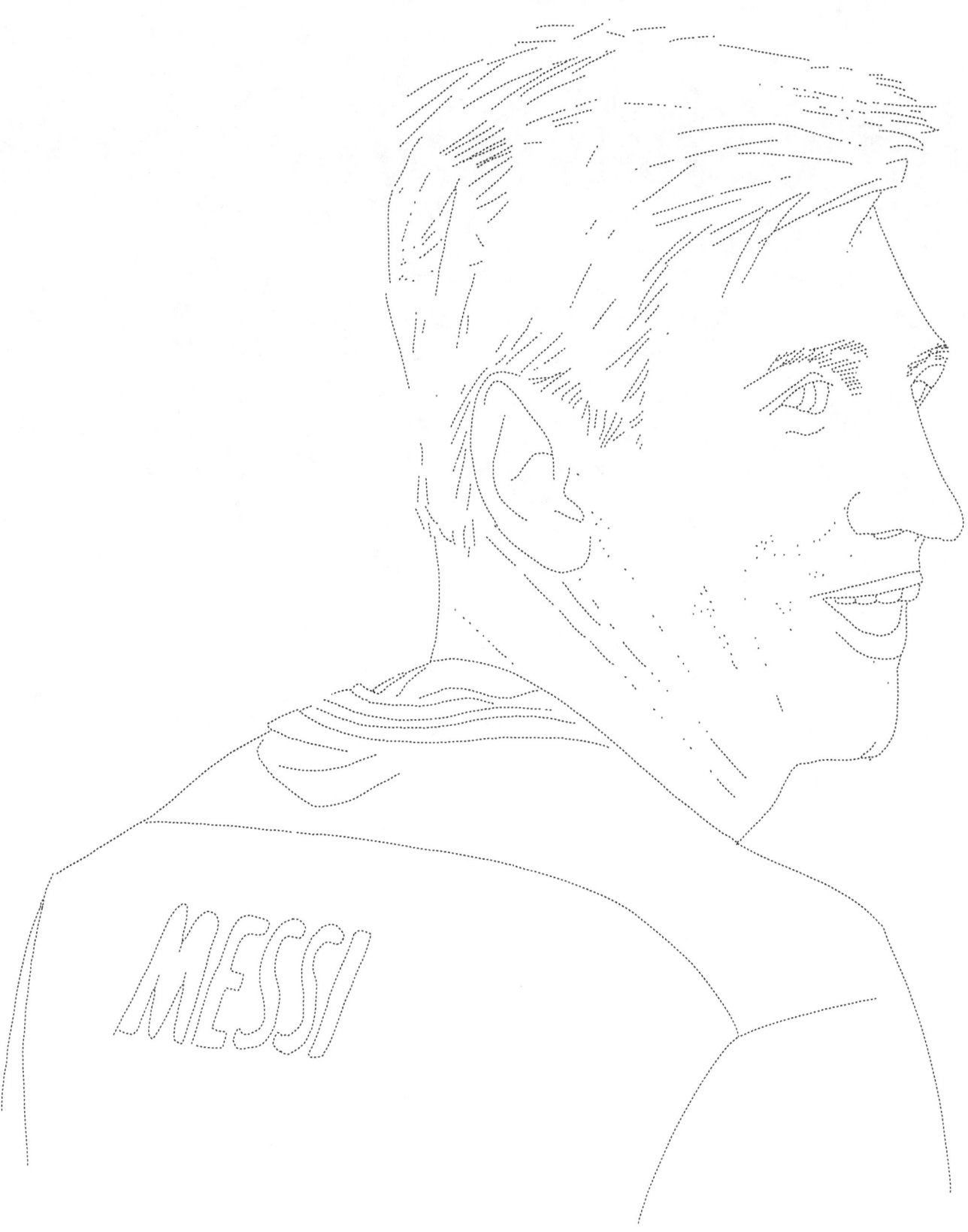

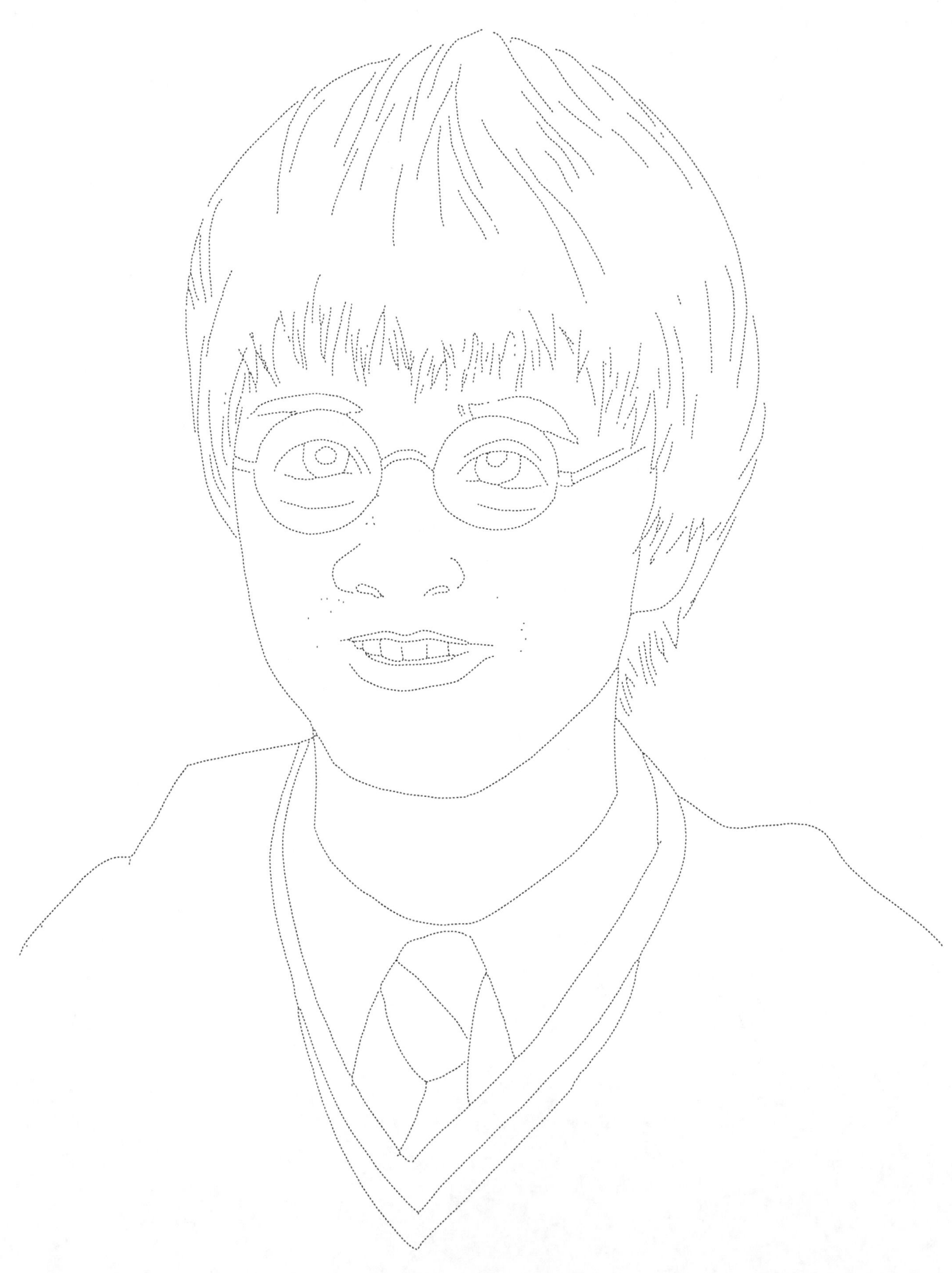

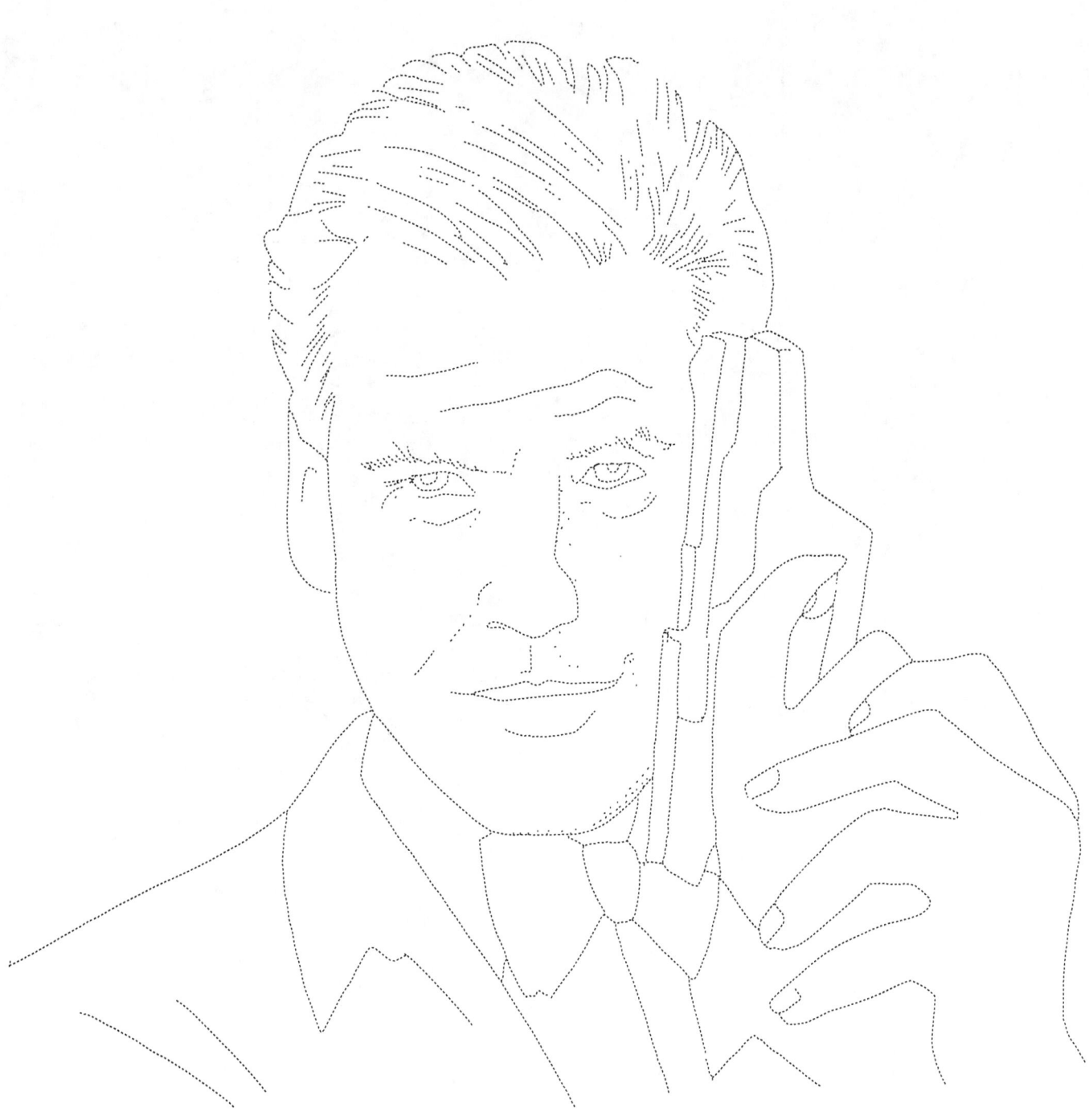

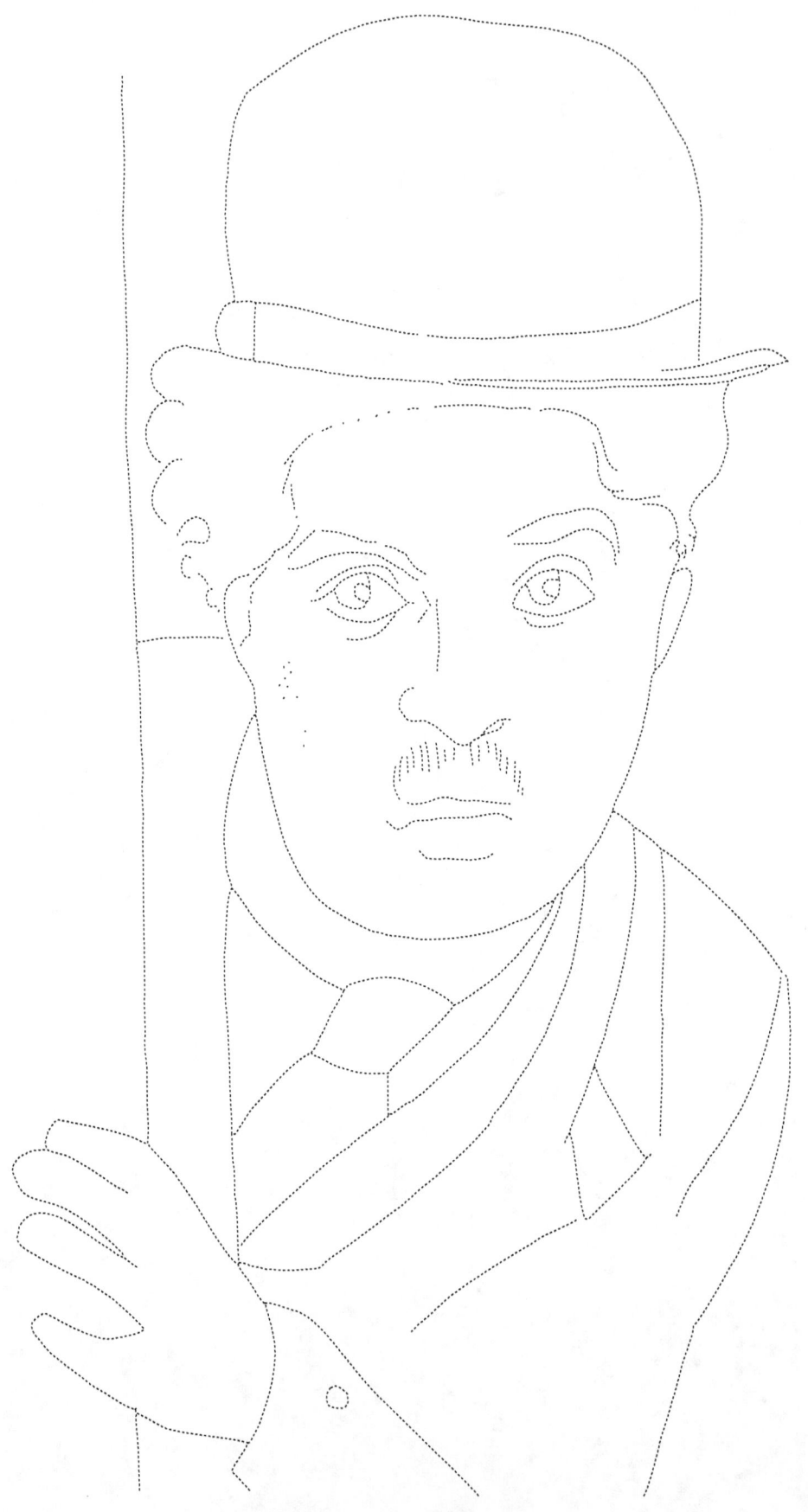

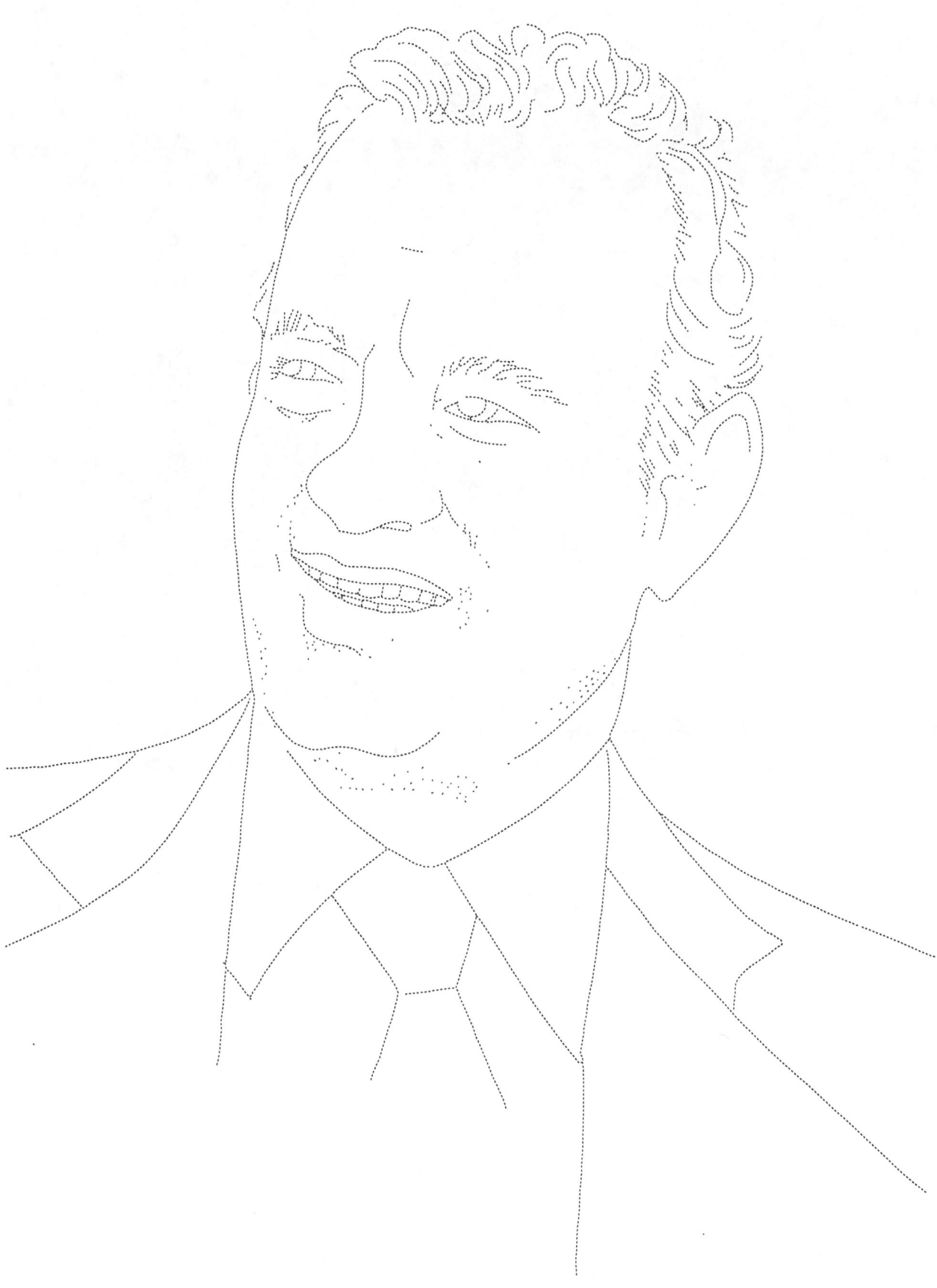

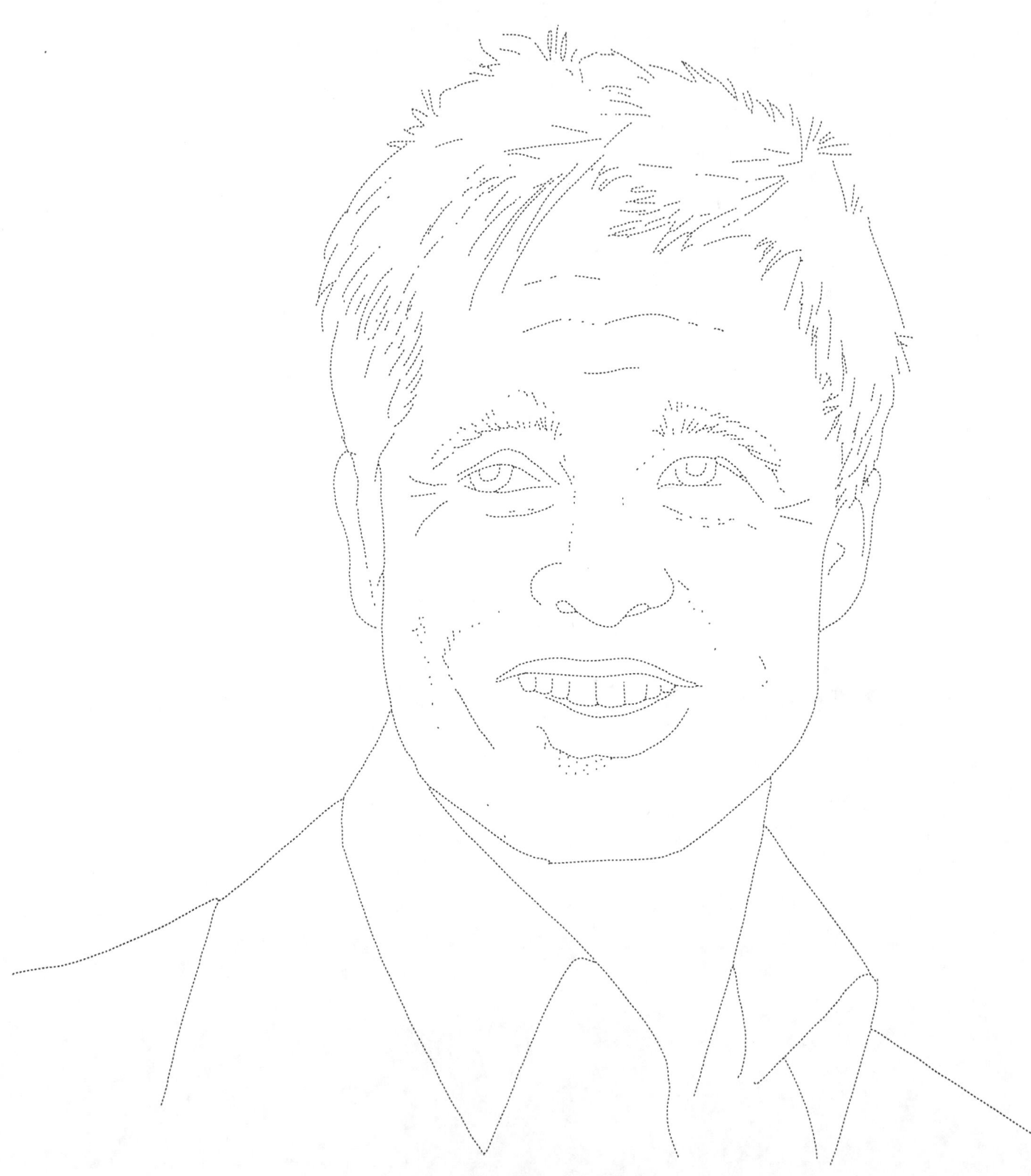

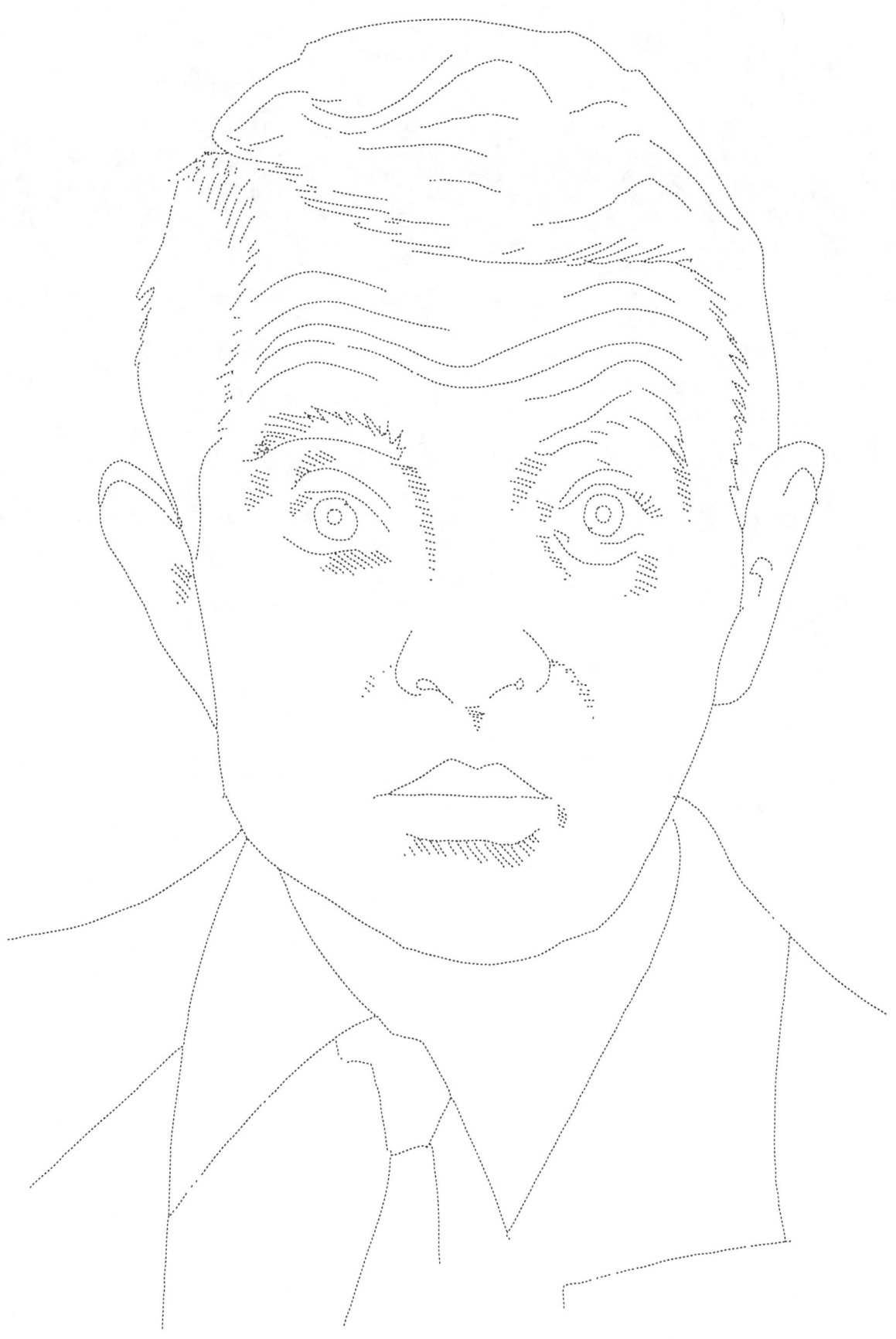

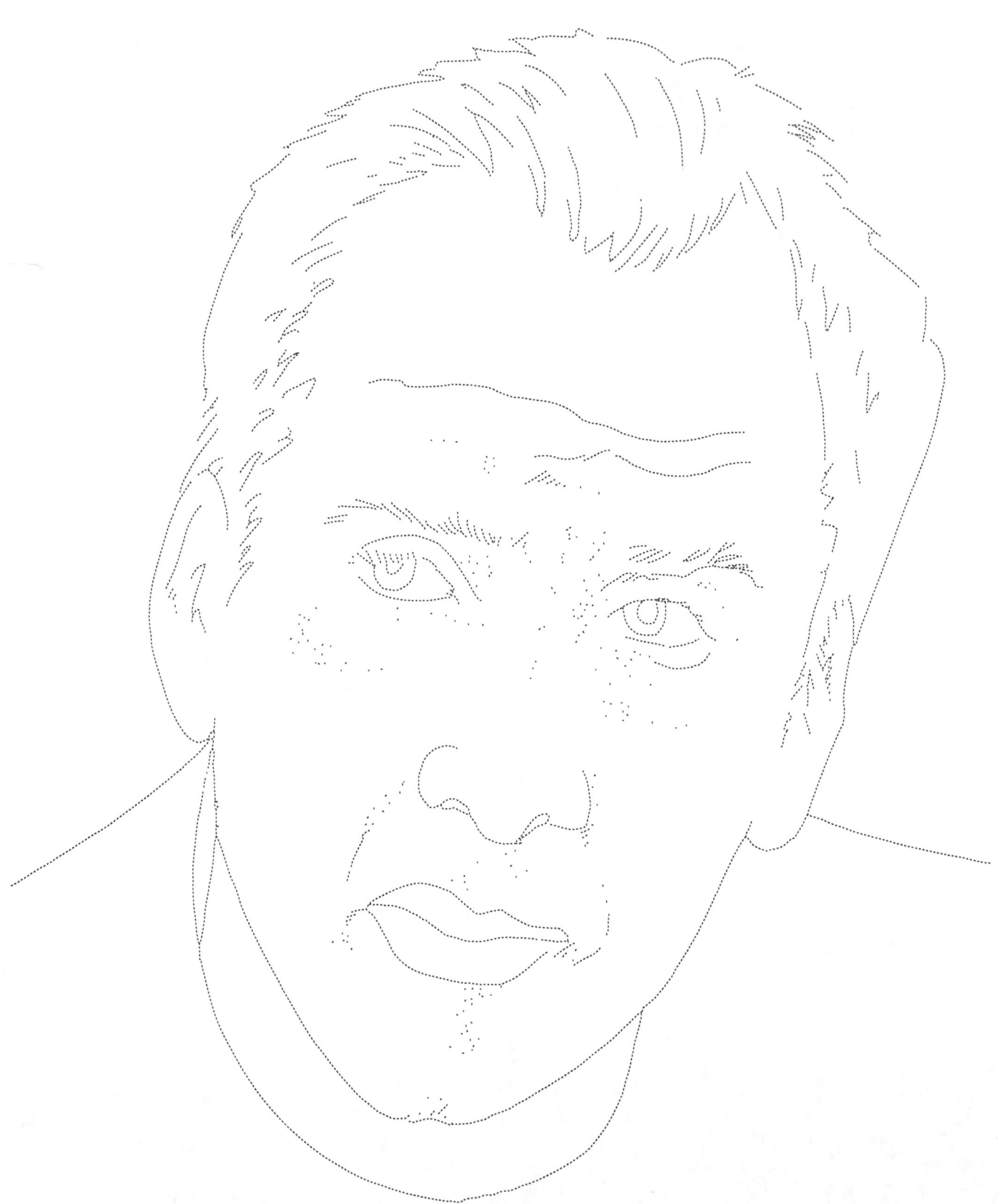

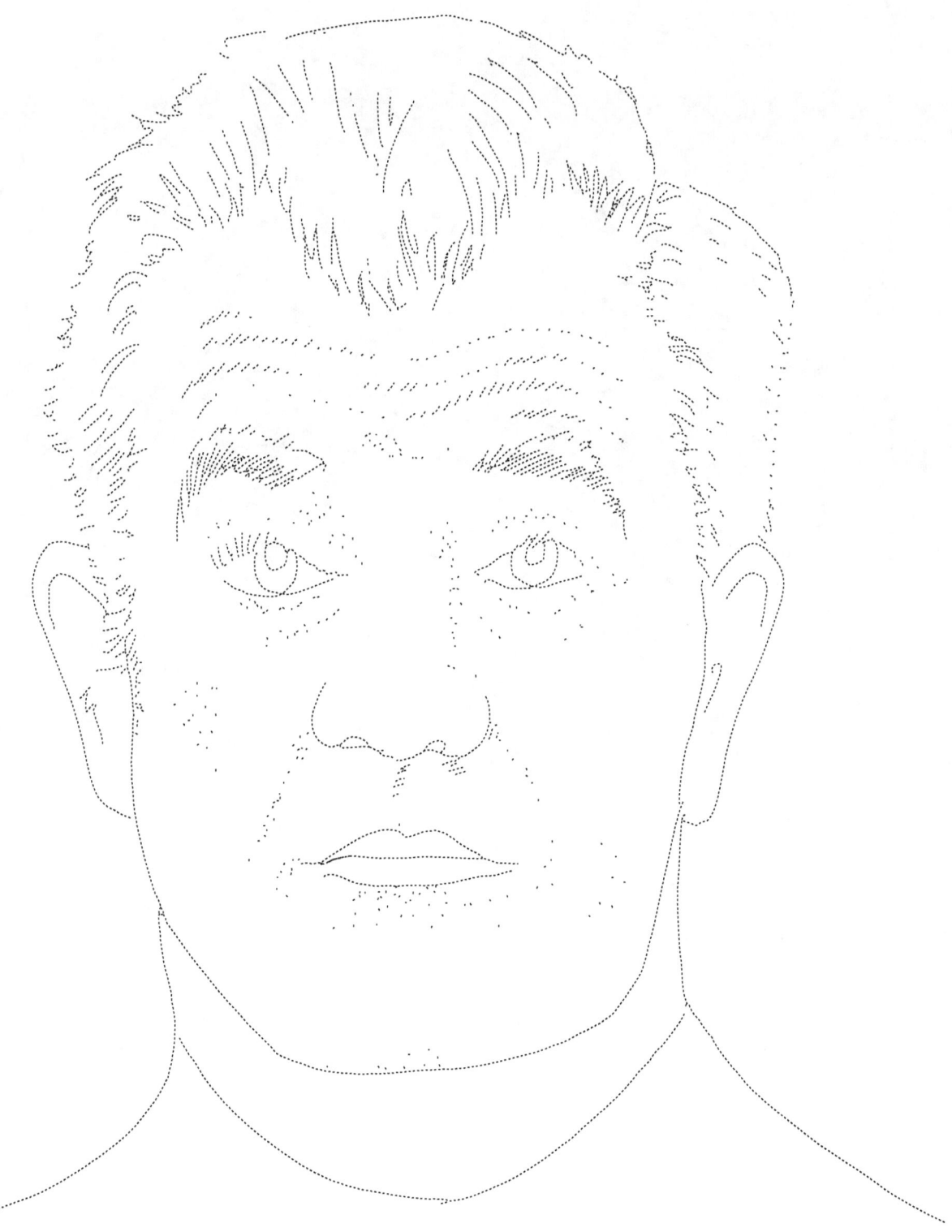

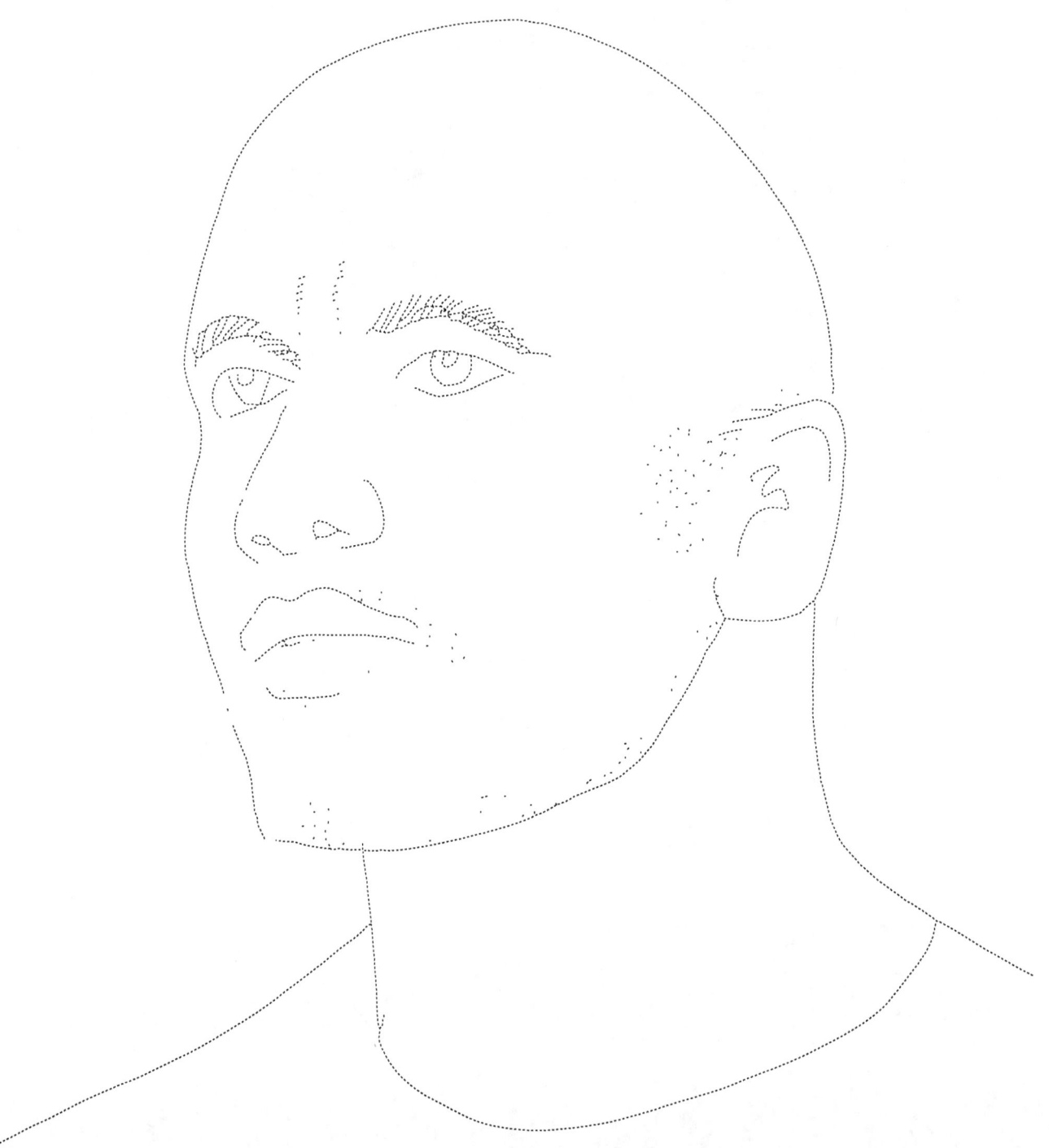

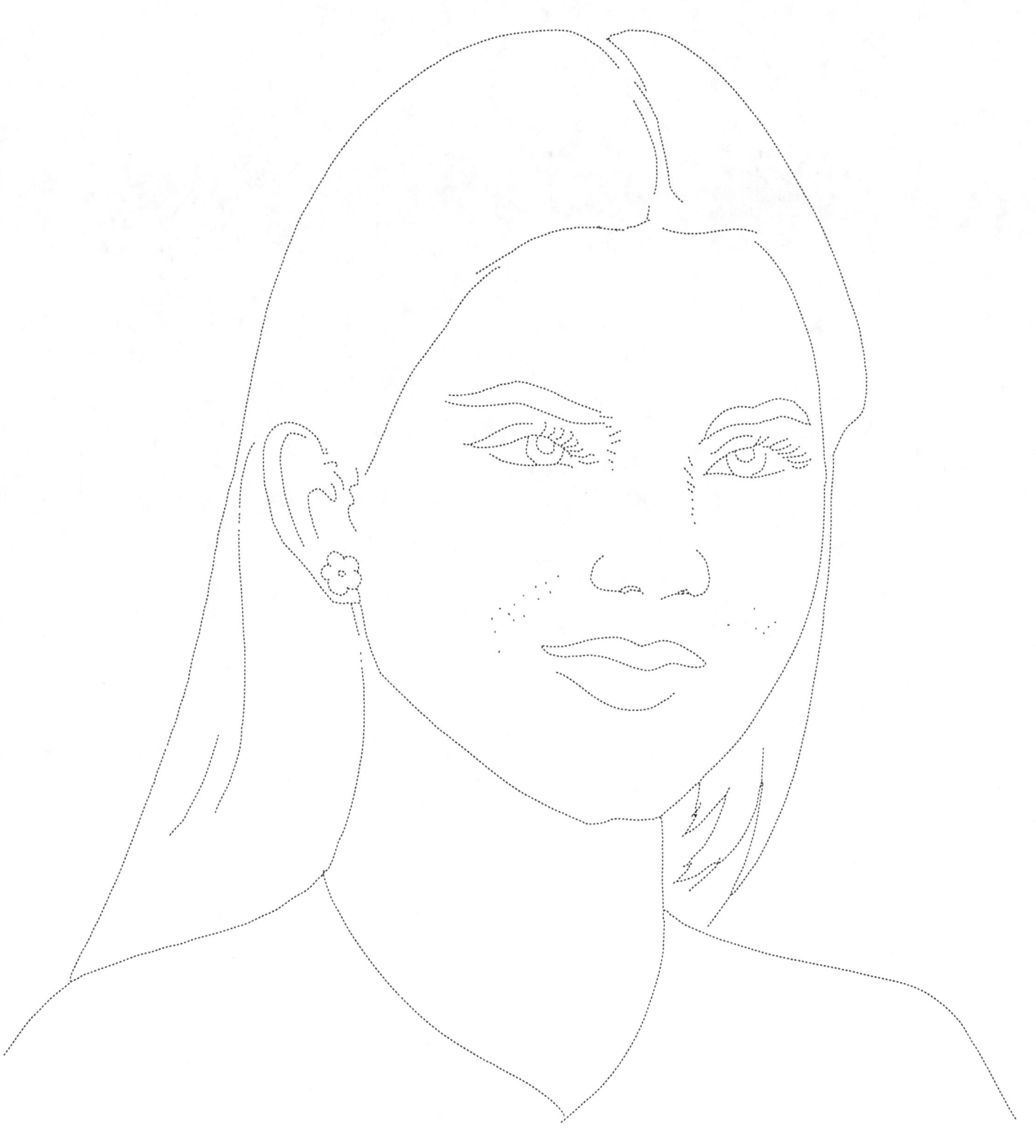

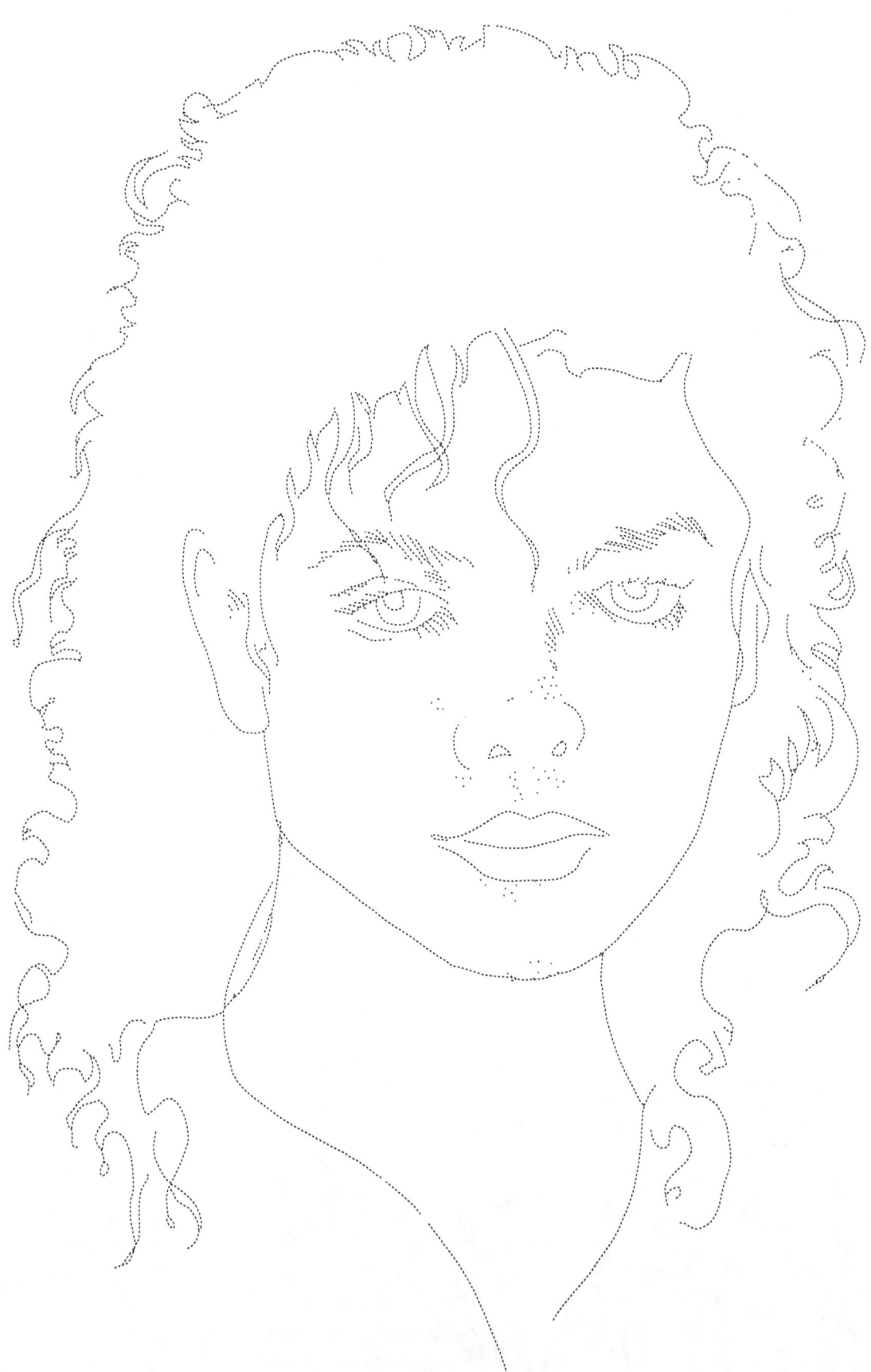

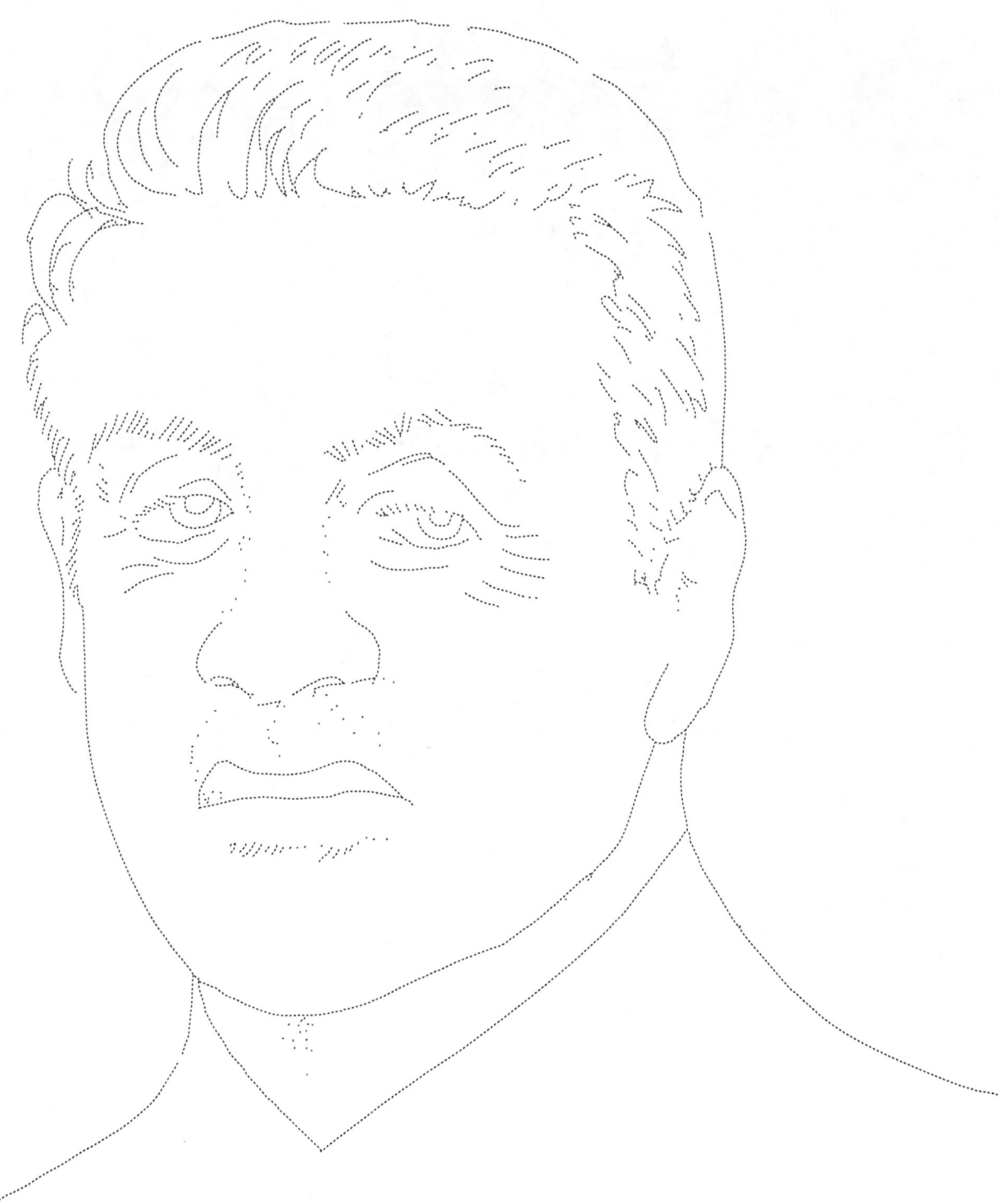

47

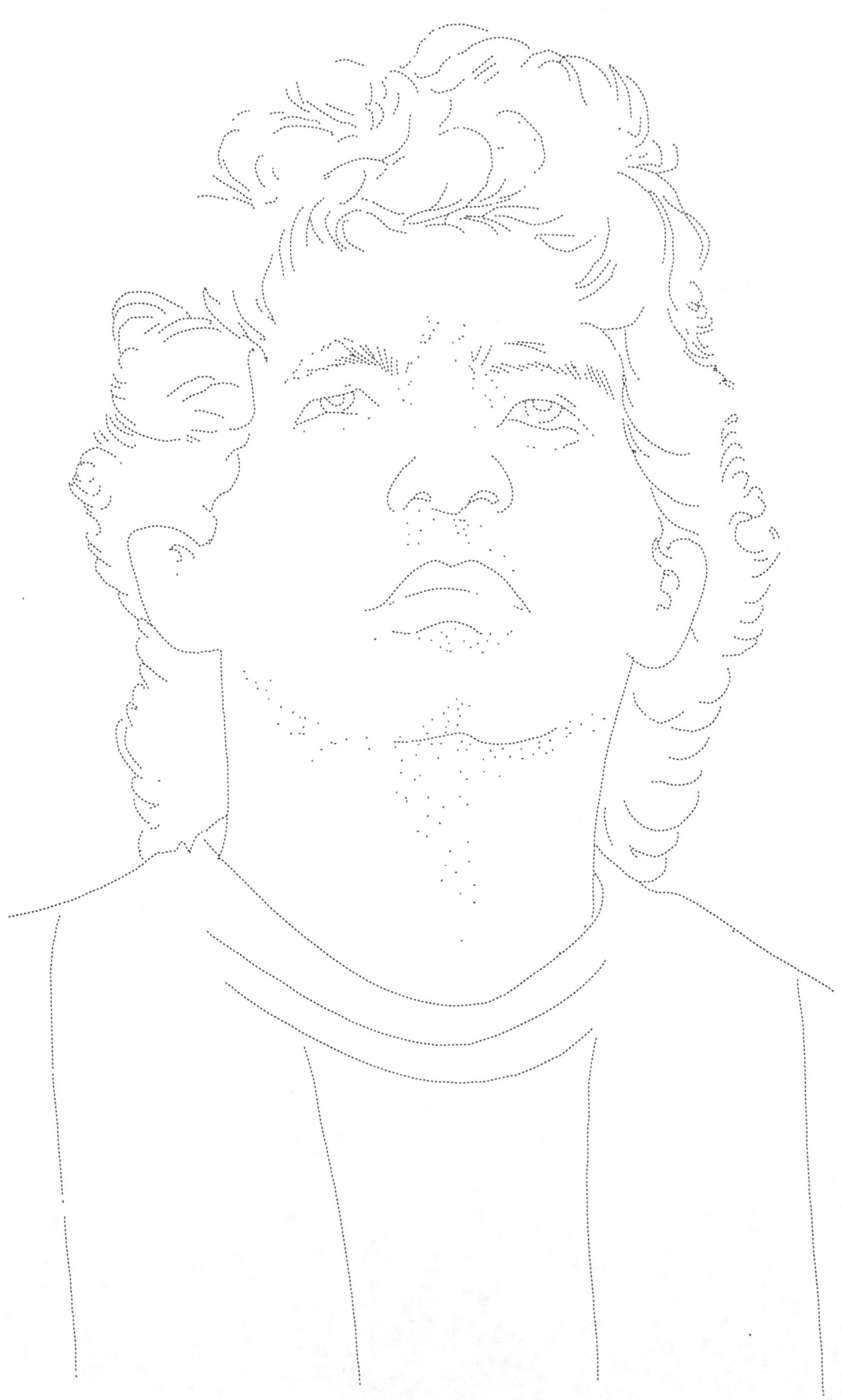

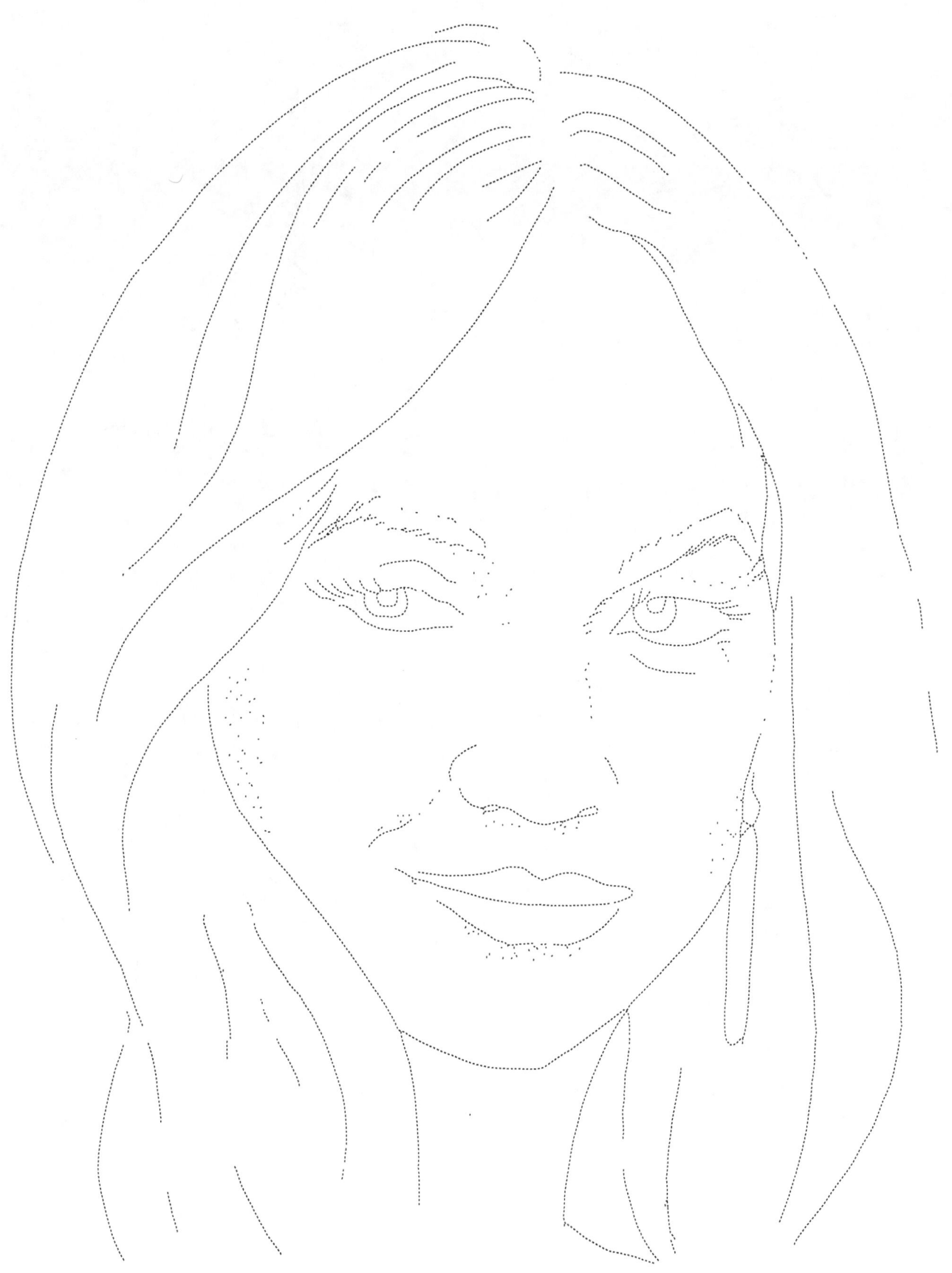

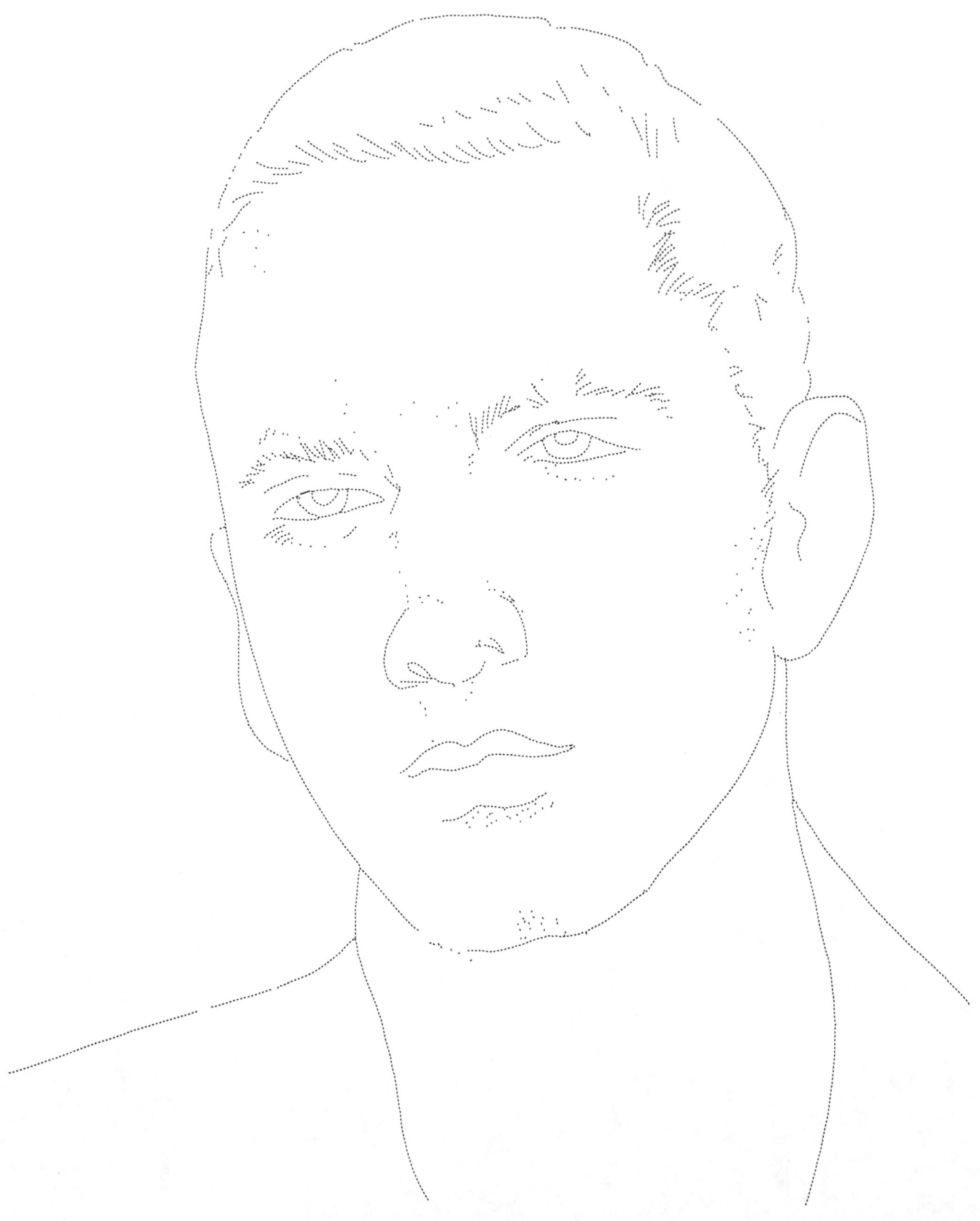

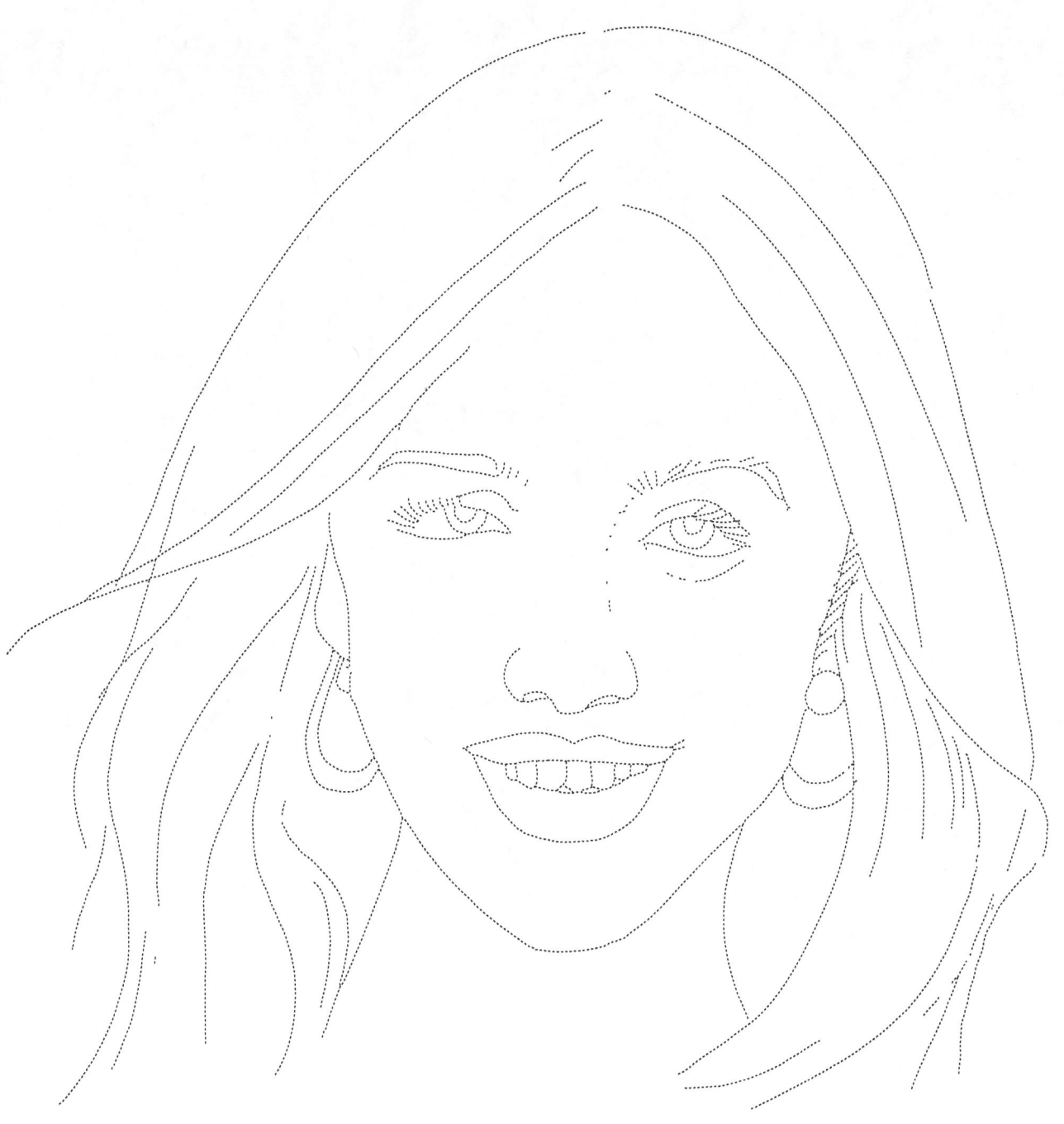

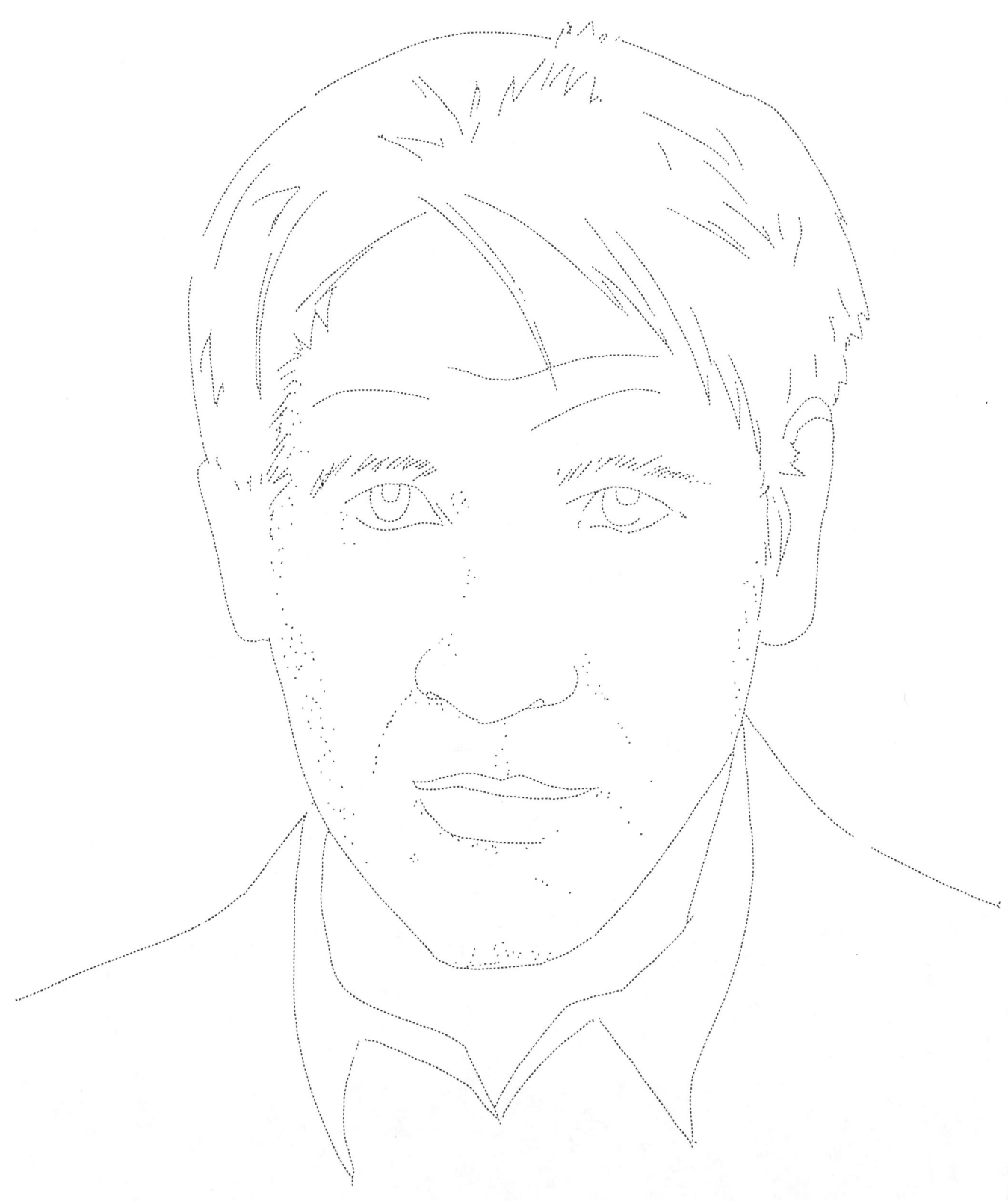

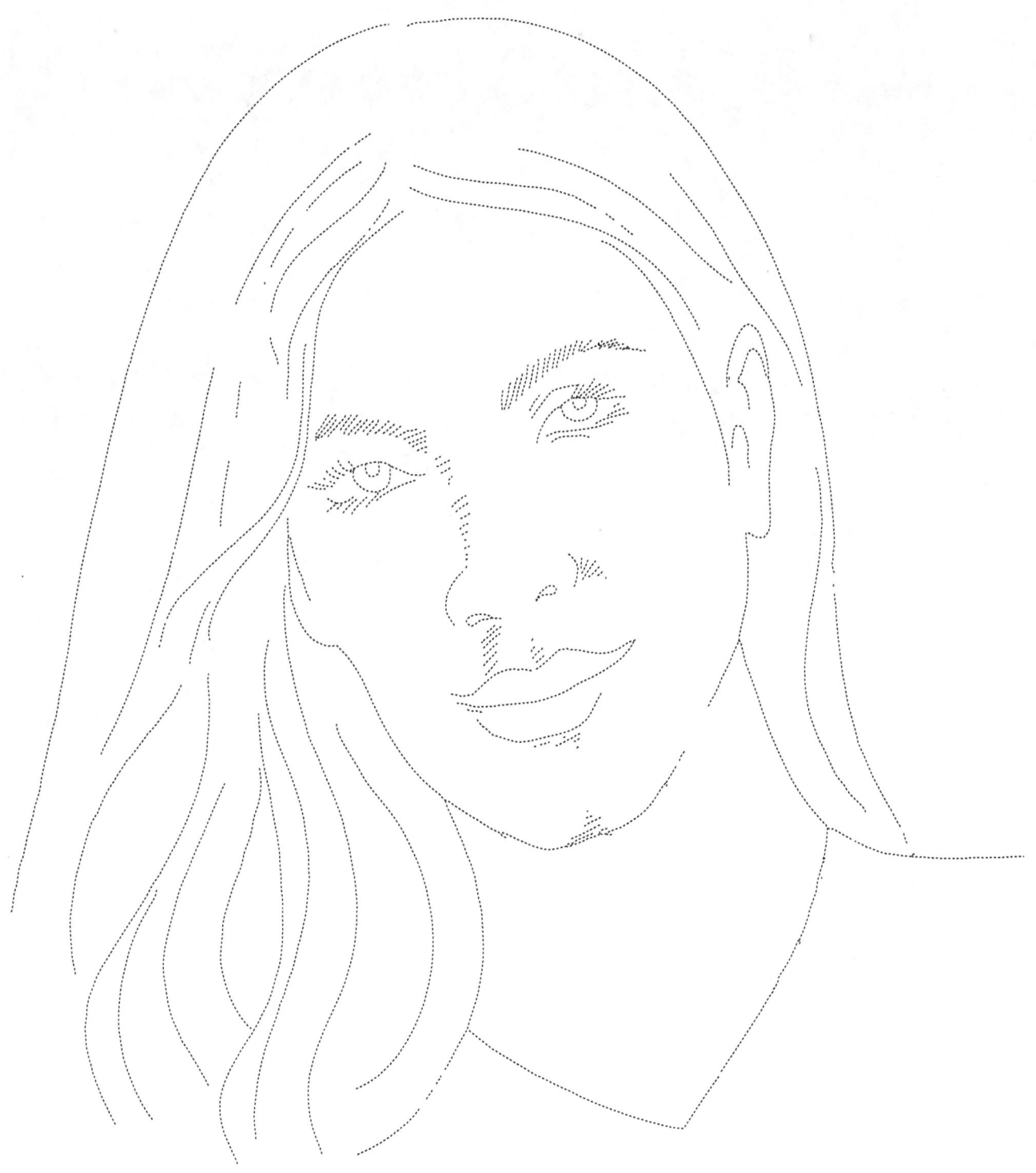

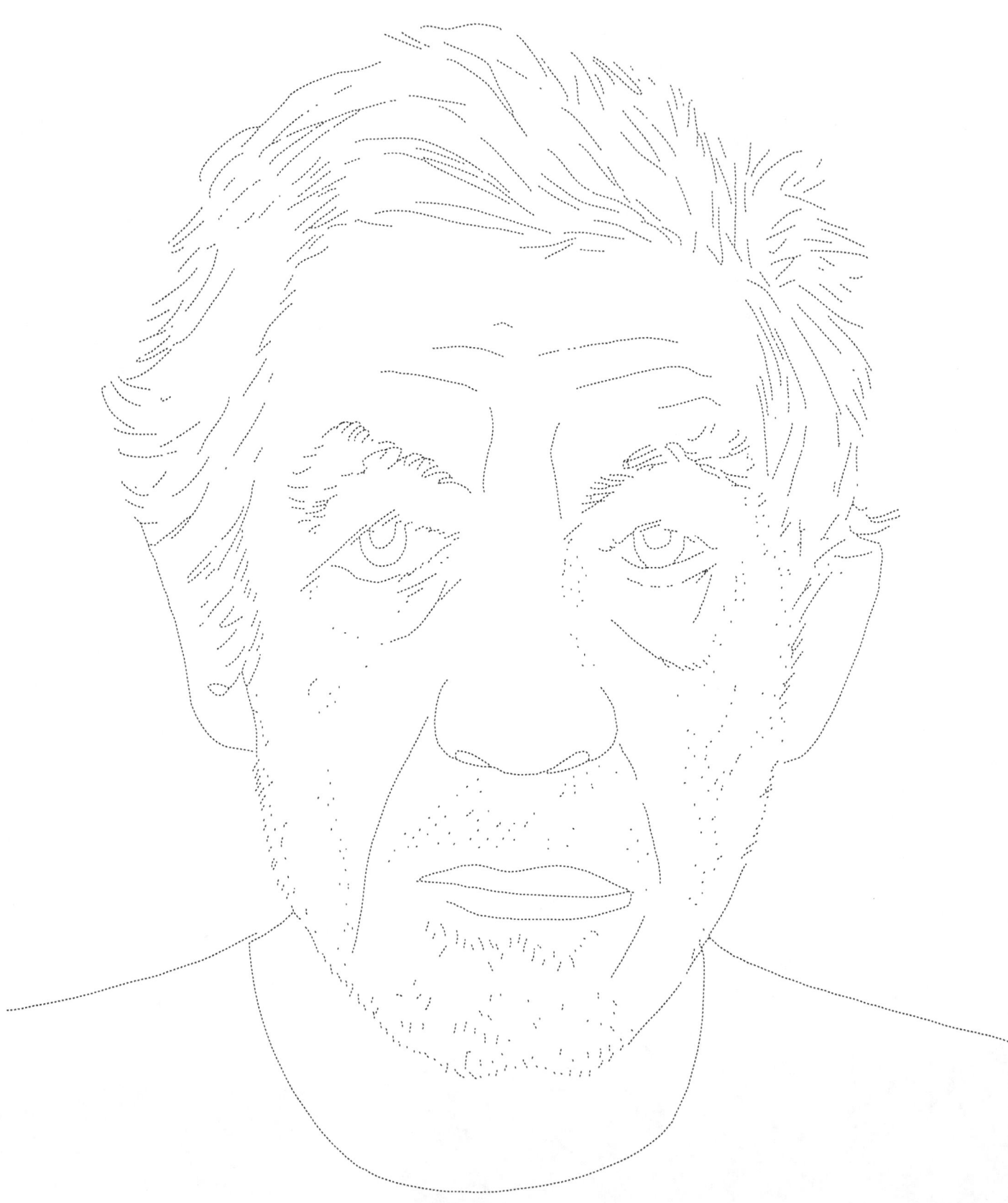

54

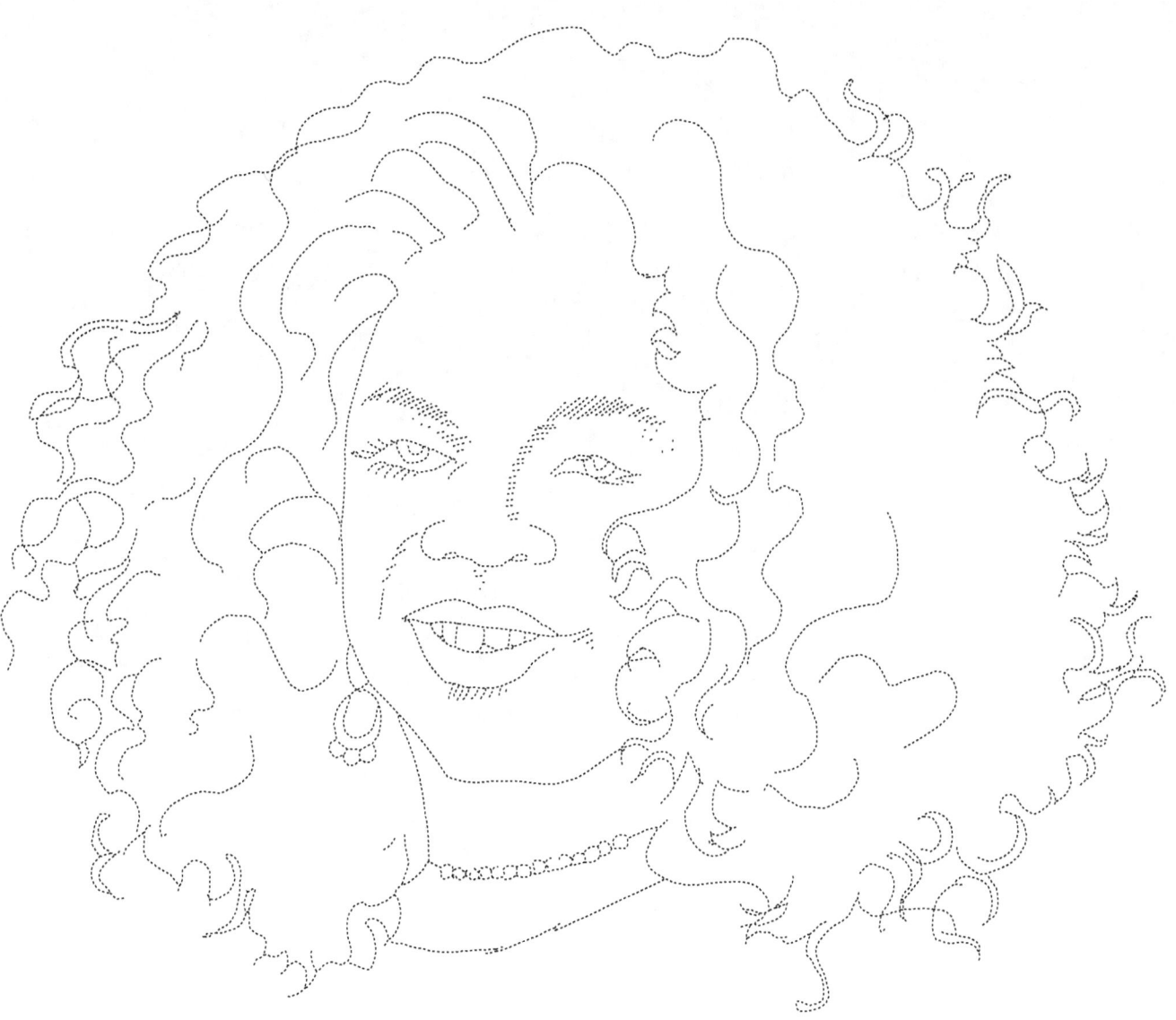

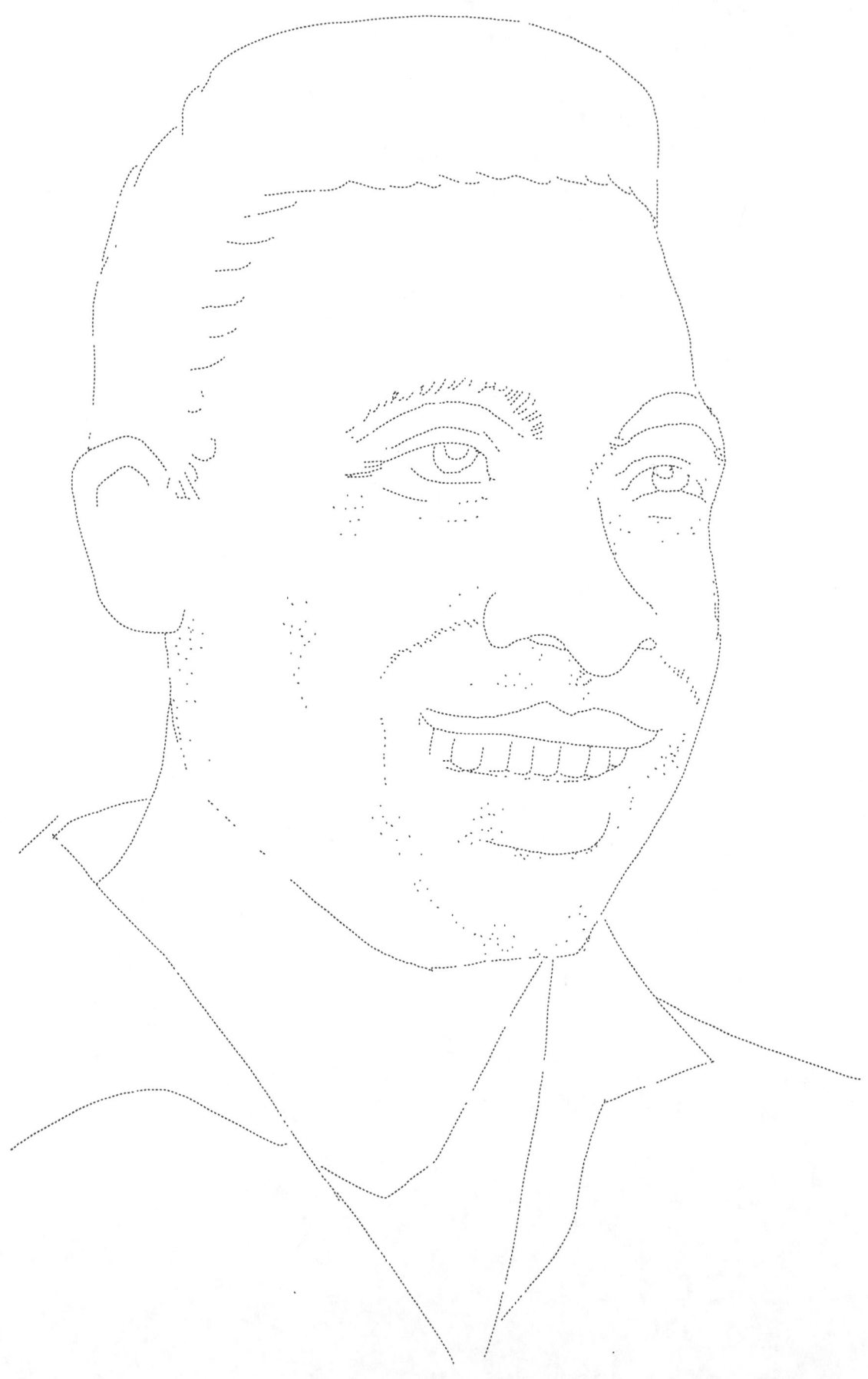

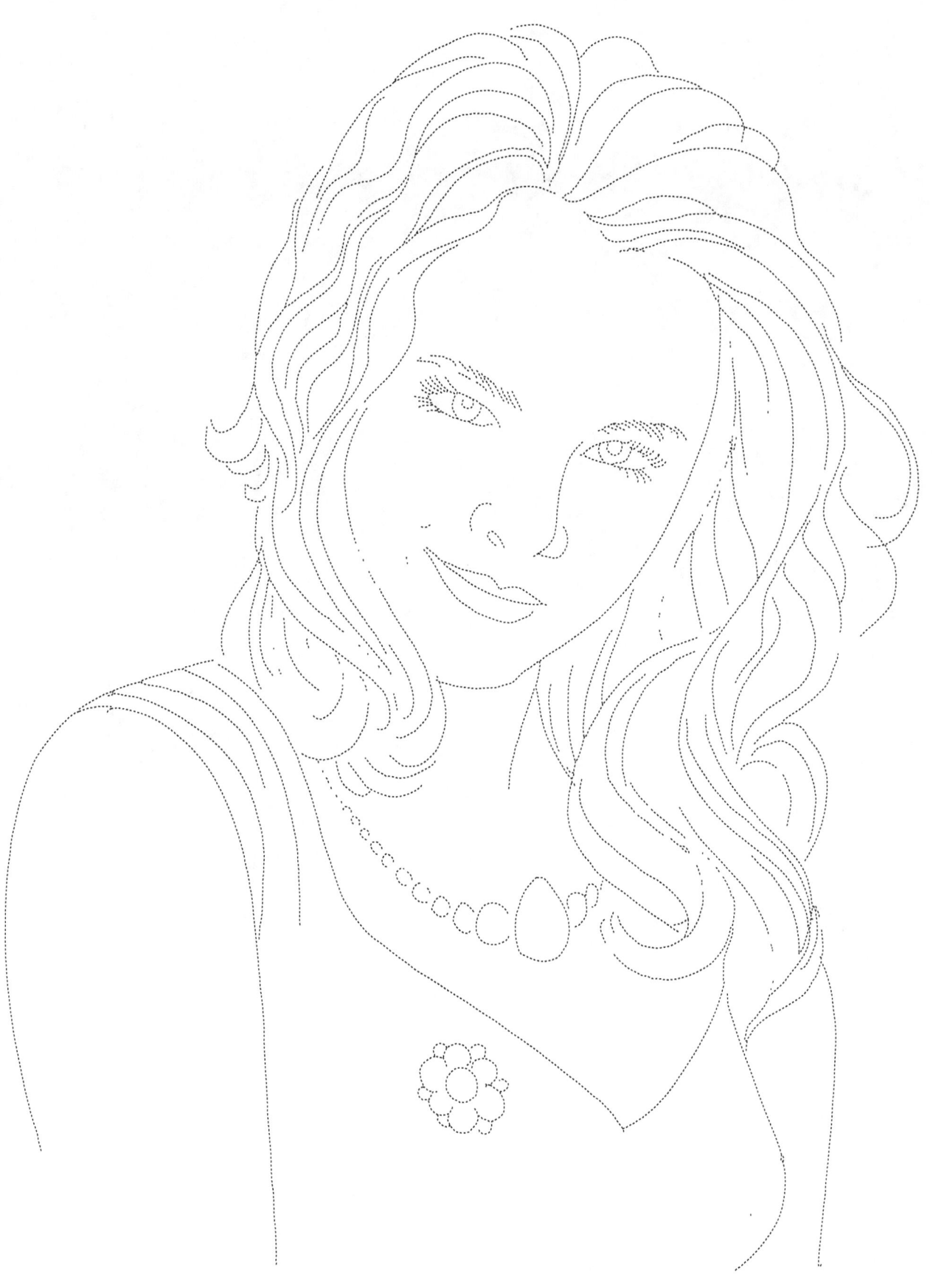

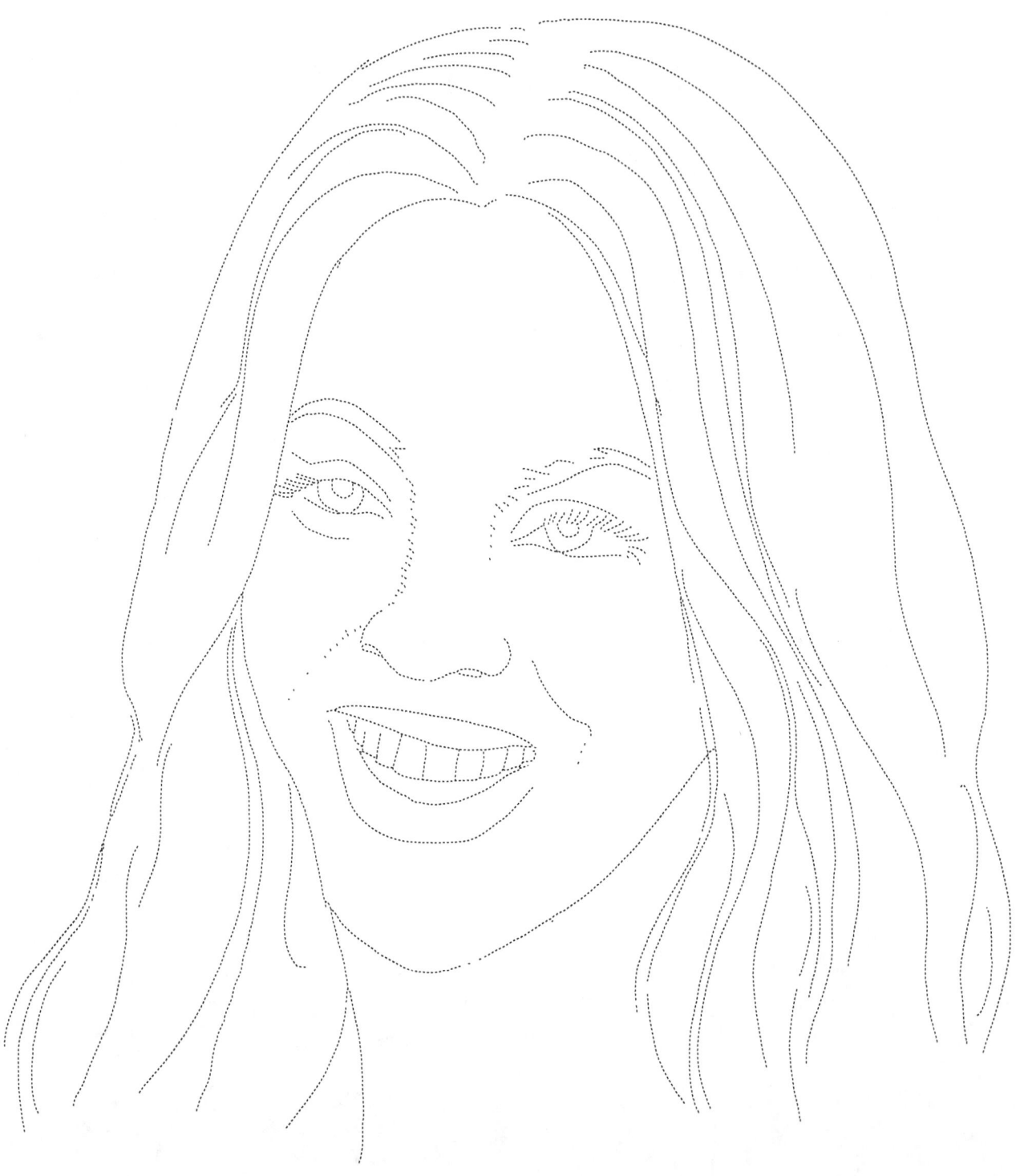

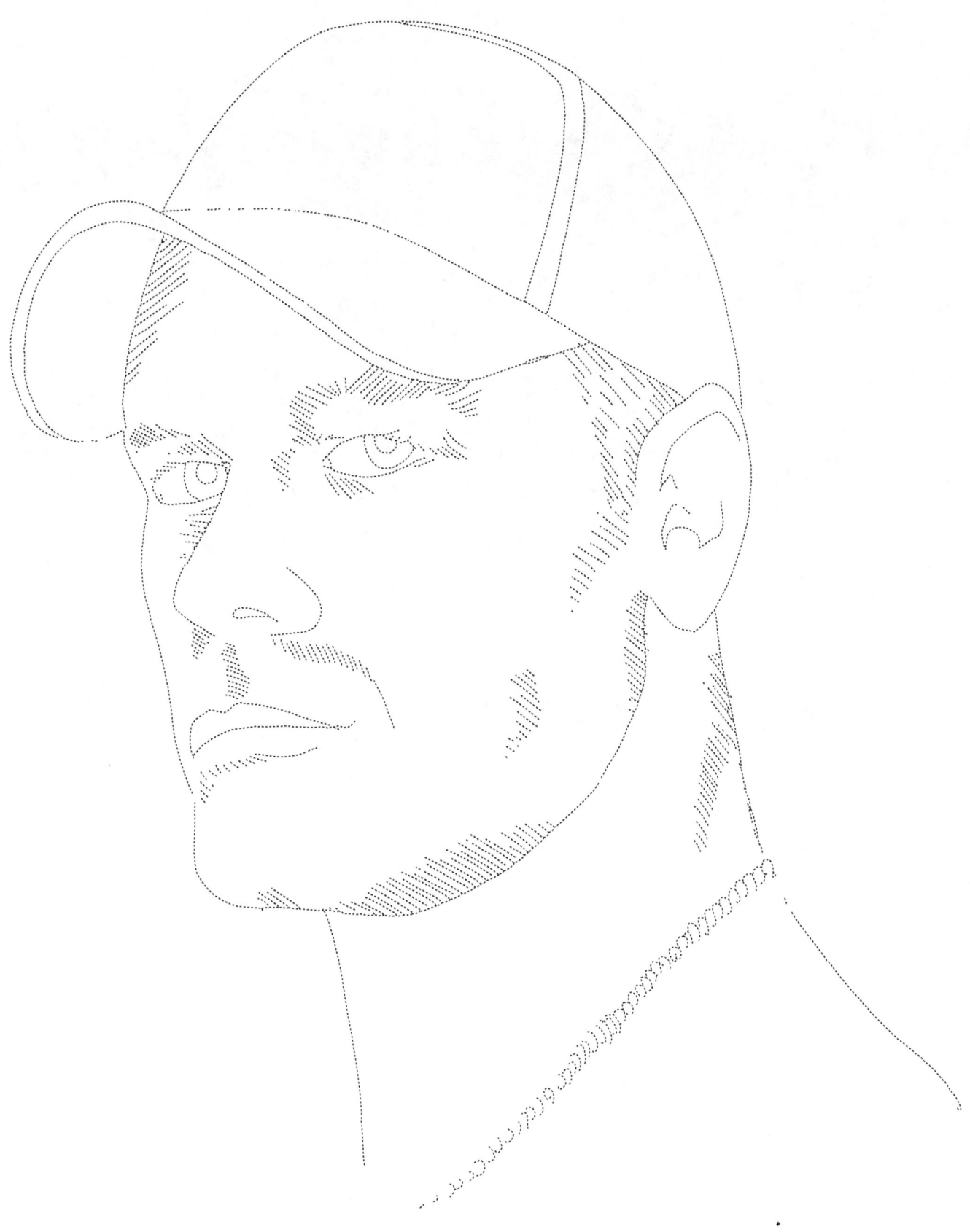

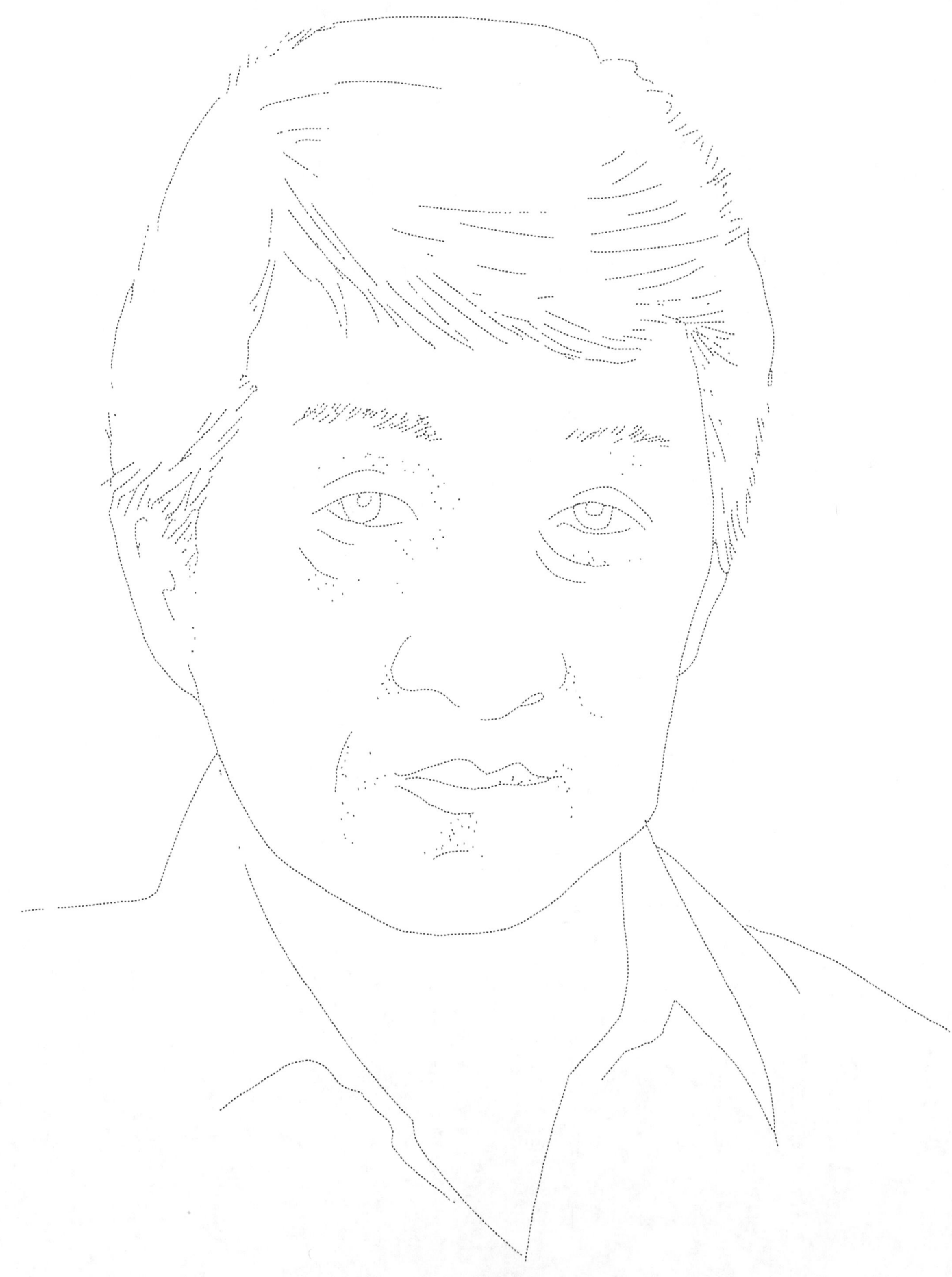

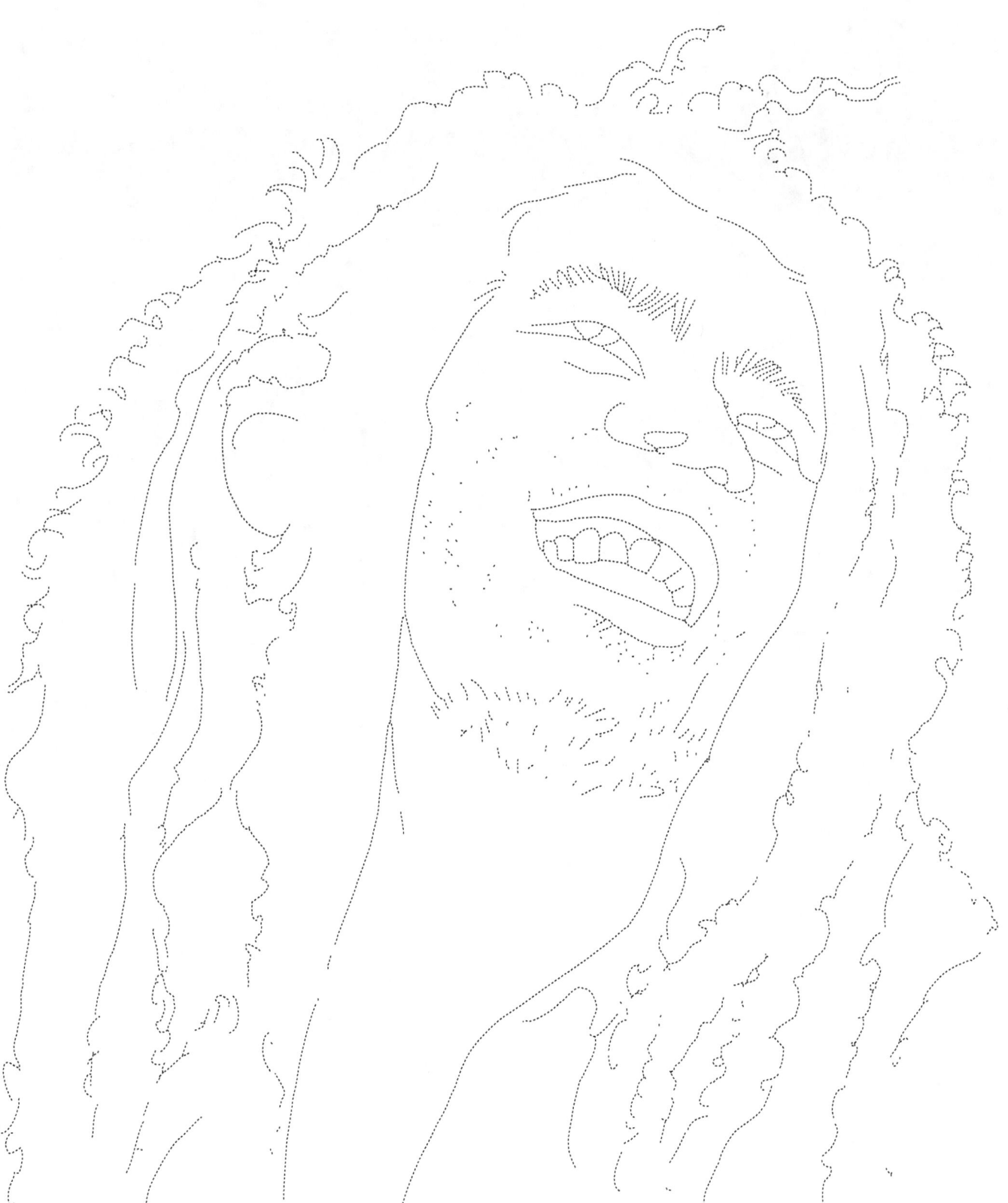

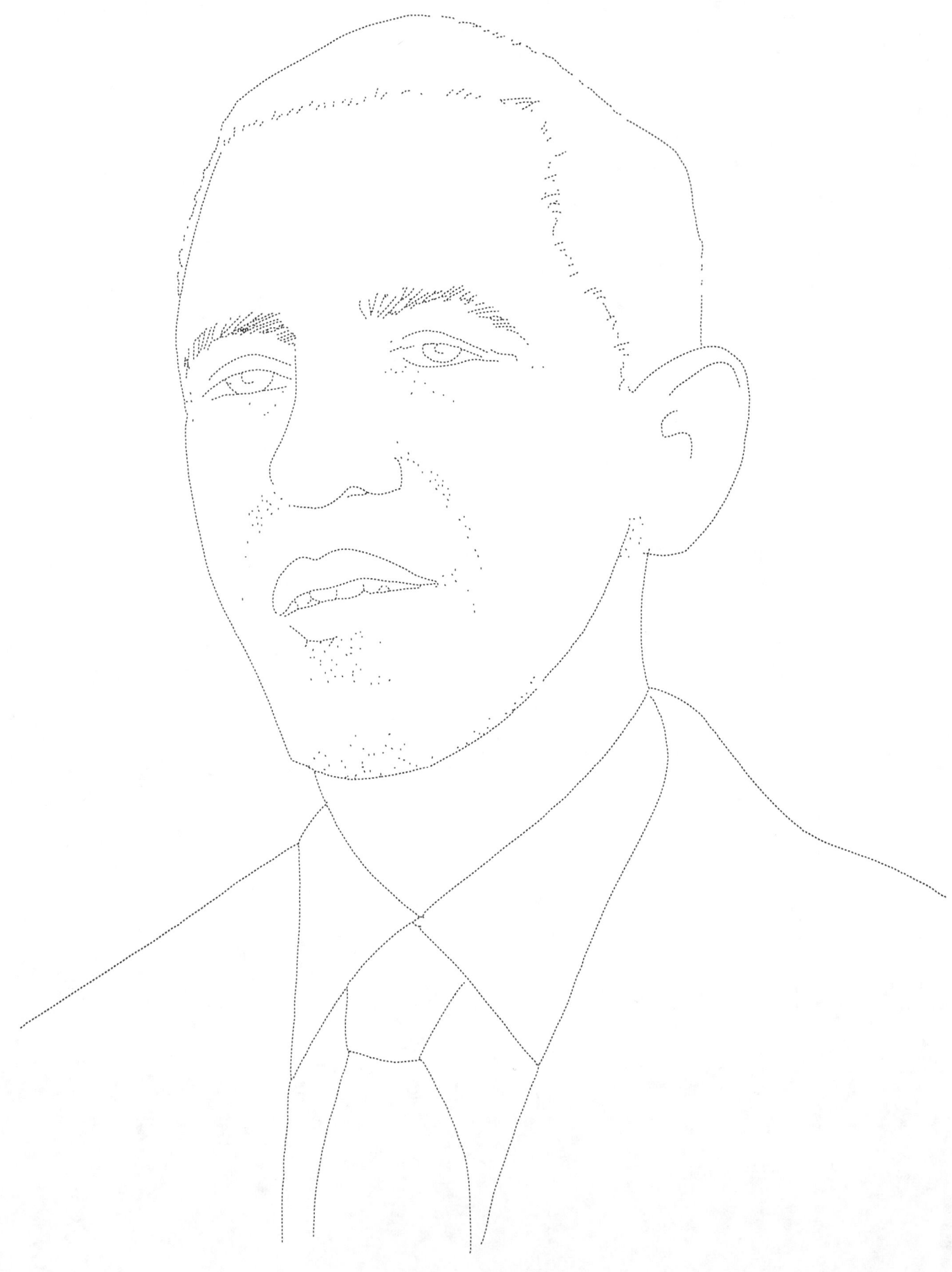

62